01

CAMERA BAG COMPANIONS™

Digital SLR Shooting Tips

CIDER MILL PRESS
BOOK PUBLISHERS

CIDER MILL PRESS
BOOK PUBLISHERS

Visit us on the web at
www.cidermillpress.com
or write to us at
12 Port Farm Road
Kennebunkport, Maine 04046

The Ilex Press, 210 High Street ,
Lewes, East Sussex, BN7 2NS, UK

www.ilex-press.com

Publisher: Alastair Campbell
Creative Director: Peter Bridgewater
Managing Editor: Chris Gatcum
Editor: Steve Luck
Art Director: Julie Weir
Senior Designer: Emily Harbison
Designer: Ginny Zeal

Library of Congress Cataloging-in-Publication Data:
A catalog record for this book is available from the Library of Congress.

ISBN 978-1-60433-116-5

Printed and bound in China

CONTENTS

Take the shot!

Before we embark on the more technical shooting tips, let's first cover one of the most overlooked. Throughout the history of photography, there have been countless occasions when photographers have expressed their dismay at missing a unique photo opportunity. We've all done it, and for a variety of reasons, but actually not having a camera is really the only truly valid one.

In many ways a digital camera, with its multitude of menus and modes, encourages tweaking and fiddling, but don't be tempted to adjust the ISO, check the white balance, or set the image size if you know the scene in front of you is "the moment." If in any doubt at all, set the camera to Full Auto and fire.

Customize your settings

Alternatively many DSLRs now allow you to customize your own shooting settings. If you're keen on reportage or street photography, for example, program into the camera the various parameters you know work best for that style of photography, such as ISO 400, shutter speed 1/125 sec, aperture f/8, file format RAW, file size large. That way you'll know that with a flick of a switch you'll have workable settings that are likely to get you a useable shot.

This shot of two young puppies playing on the beach was taken without giving a second thought to lighting, background, or exposure setting; and so more by luck than judgement a unique moment in time (as well as a picture of some cute puppies) has been captured in perpetuity.

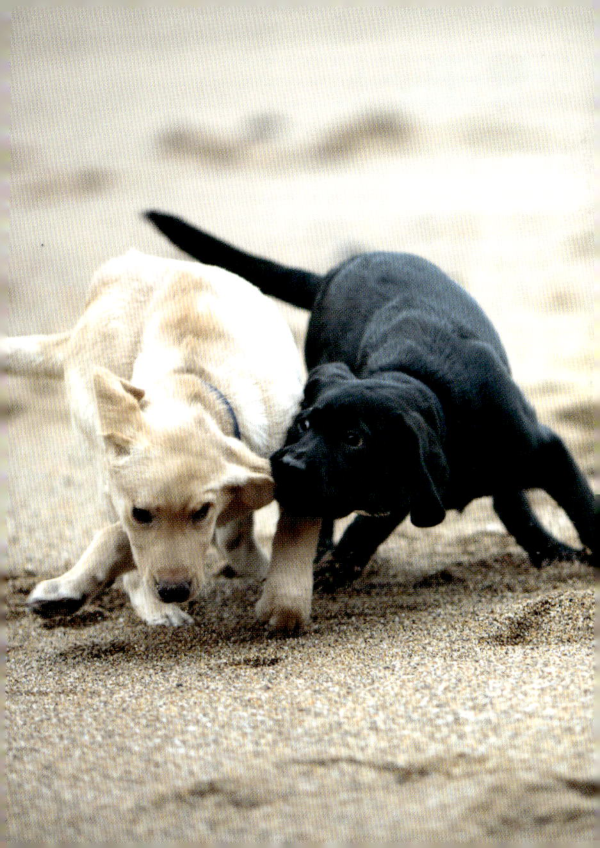

Sensitivity: ISO settings

Along with the shutter speed and aperture setting, a digital camera's ISO setting can also be adjusted to ensure an accurate exposure. Every time the ISO setting is doubled, the amount of light needed to create a perfectly exposed picture is halved. This means that if you shift from using ISO 100 to ISO 200 you can use a shutter speed that is twice as fast, or open the aperture by a full stop. Shift from ISO 100 to ISO 1600, and you can use a shutter speed that is 16 times faster than before, or open up the aperture by four stops. In other words, being able to alter the camera sensor's sensitivity allows you much more creative control with either the shutter speed or aperture. But with higher ISO settings comes more noise.

Choosing the right ISO value

ISO value	Speed	Noise	Applications
50–100	Slow	Low	Daylight photography. Low light with flash. Any photograph where a solid tripod can be used.
200–400	Medium	Medium	Hand held camera in low light with fast shutter speed. Smaller aperture than would otherwise be used in current lighting conditions without a tripod. Increase effective range of flash.
800–6400	Fast	High	Hand held camera in lowest lighting conditions where flash is not being used or where subject is out of flash range. Examples: Museum exhibits, candid portraits, indoor parties, architectural interiors where tripods are not allowed.

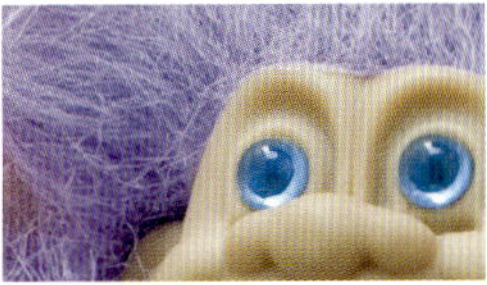

ISO 100—THE CAMERA'S NATIVE SENSITIVITY

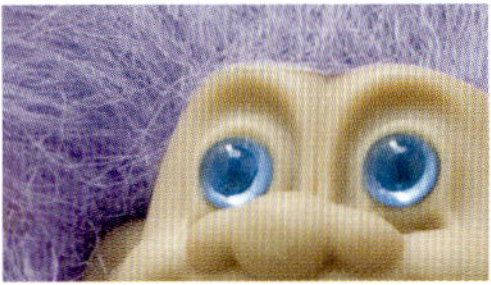

ISO 200

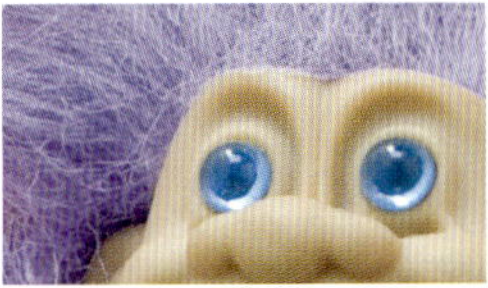

ISO 400

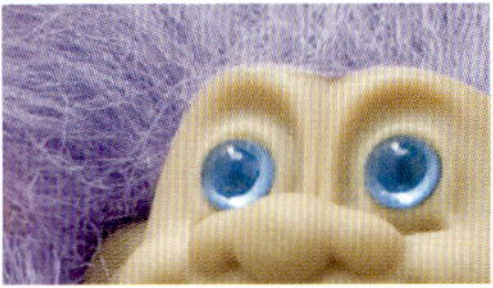

ISO 800

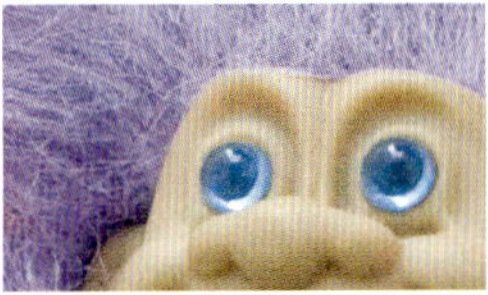

ISO 6400

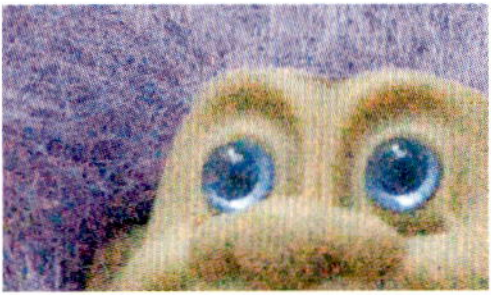

ISO 25,600

The series of images above demonstrates how noise becomes more apparent as ISO sensitivity is increased. Compare the images with ISO set at 100 and those at higher settings. ISO 25,600 is available only on a few cameras, and has little practical use.

TIP

The simple rule for setting the ISO is to use the lowest possible value that you can get away with. However, it is better to settle for a slightly noisier shot than to end up with a blurred one because the shutter speed was not fast enough.

Shoot Raw

A Raw image file contains all the unprocessed data captured by the sensor at the time the photo was taken. It is unprocessed (hence "raw") in the sense that the camera doesn't apply any image enhancement in-camera, such as sharpening or contrast adjustments. While a Raw file may look distinctly "unfinished" straight out of the camera, it contains more data than either JPEG or TIFF files; so much more data that not only can you enhance the image by sharpening or improving color and contrast in a much more controlled and selective way, but you can also alter the overall exposure, change the white balance, and make far more radical alterations to the image without it degrading than would be possible with a JPEG or TIFF file. Having a Raw version of your image is like keeping a master negative, as you can go back to make new and different versions of the same image, safe in the knowledge that your original data will always be available.

The biggest drawback to Raw files is that you have to process them manually to get a useable image file, and that takes time. With JPEGs and TIFFs you can set the level of color saturation, contrast, sharpening, and more, in camera; and as long as the scene is well exposed, you'll end up with an excellent image that's comparable with a carefully processed Raw file.

When to use JPEGs or TIFFS

As a rule of thumb, therefore, for family or holiday snaps (without wanting to diminish their value) a JPEG is likely to provide you with excellent results (as is a TIFF, but these take up more space on the memory card). For your "works of art," however, particularly those taken in difficult lighting situations, shooting Raw will provide you with the best possible data for making the most of the image.

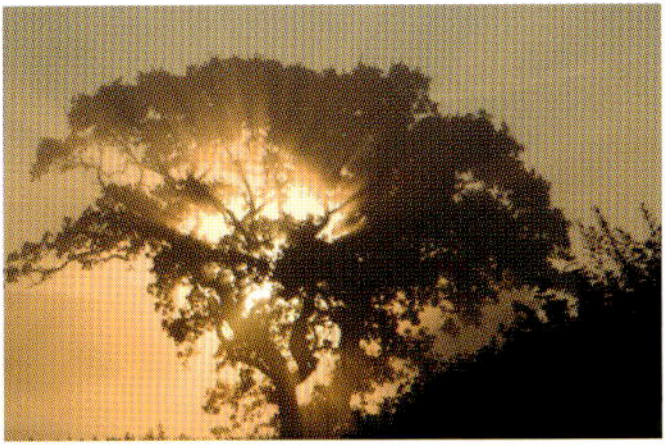

Shooting Raw gives you much greater control over image adjustment than shooting JPEGs or TIFFs. Here, for example, the white balance and exposure are easily adjusted without degrading the image.

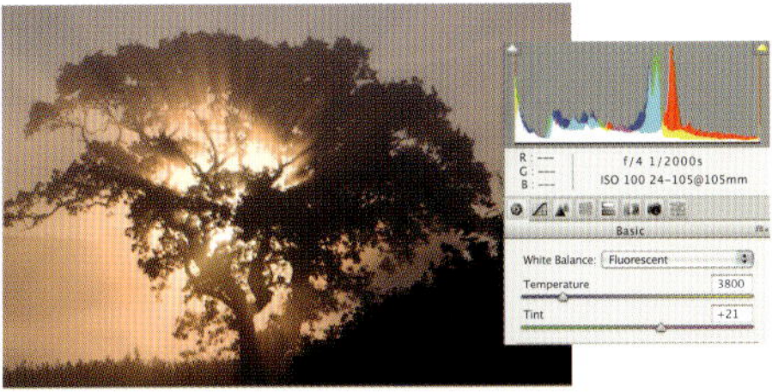

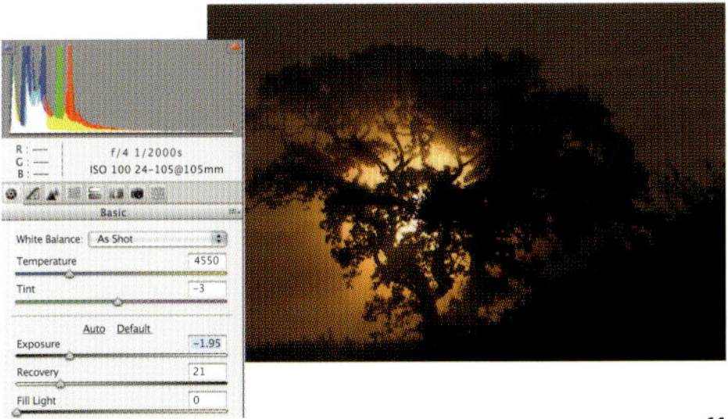

Focus lock

Modern DSLRs have very sophisticated autofocusing (AF) systems, which make our photographic lives much easier. However, there will be times when the camera is either unable to focus on a subject (perhaps due to lack of contrast) or the subject is not in the center of the viewfinder, where the default focus points are usually located, and you want to photograph him or her off-center. While more sophisticated cameras allow you to change the focus point to one that covers the subject, it's usually quicker and easier to use focus lock; while in other cases, the camera's central focus point may be more sensitive and respond better in low-light conditions and so is the best one to use.

Simply focus on the subject using the center focus point by depressing the shutter release halfway. Next recompose the shot while still semi-depressing the release button; this will tell the camera to hold the original focus. When you're happy with the composition fire the shutter.

This technique will usually provide good results, but be wary of two things. First, make sure that the subject is the same distance from the camera when you recompose the shot otherwise it will no longer be in focus. Second, check that your specific camera doesn't also lock the exposure setting at the same time it locks the focus. This may result in a poorly exposed shot.

In the first shot of a young girl on an inflatable whale, the central focus point was used to ensure sharp focus and the picture was taken. In the second shot, the same central focus point was used, but this time, by semidepressing the shutter release button focus remained locked on the girl. The photographer was then able to recompose the shot for a more dynamic result, without running the risk of focusing on the sea behind her.

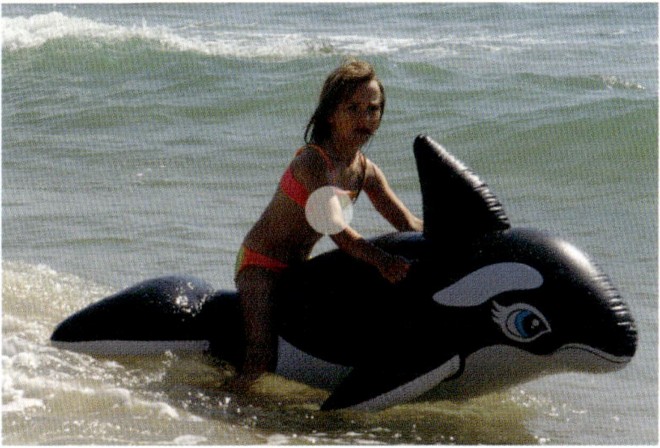

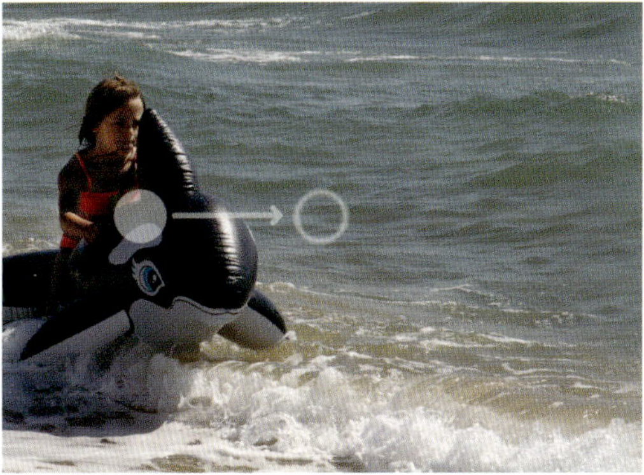

Focus: Continuous and Predictive

When shooting stationary subjects, such as portraits or landscapes, for example, the camera's one-shot or single-frame shooting mode is perfectly adequate. However, what happens if you're trying to photograph a moving subject? Most cameras now feature a form of continuous autofocus (AF), in which the camera is constantly focusing on the subject while the shutter button is pressed halfway. As long as you track your subject so that it remains over the selected focusing point, when you press the shutter it will be in focus.

However, if you're photographing a relatively fast-moving object head on from a close distance, such as a cyclist, the time it takes for the camera to fire the shutter—although a fraction of a second—is sufficiently long for the cyclist to move out of focus.

To prevent this, more sophisticated cameras have predictive autofocus (AF). With this system, the camera assesses the speed the object is moving toward the camera and allows for the shutter delay when focusing—in other words predicting where the object is going to be the instant the photo is taken.

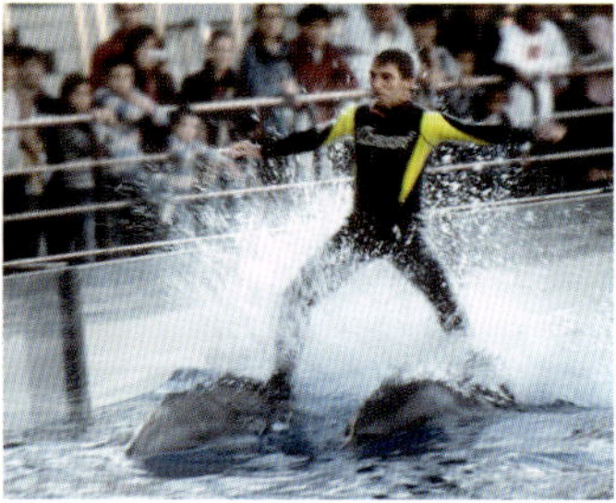

If the subject is moving across the frame, autofocus is more successful as it has less focusing adjustments to make.

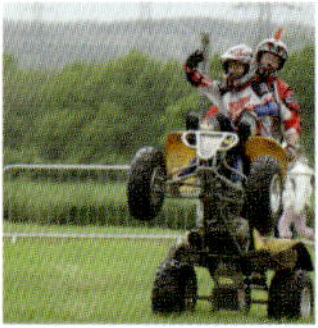
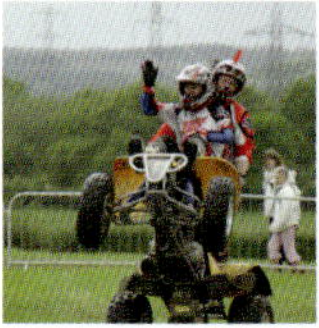
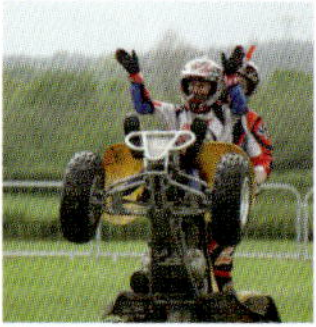
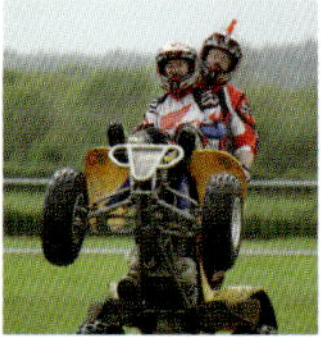
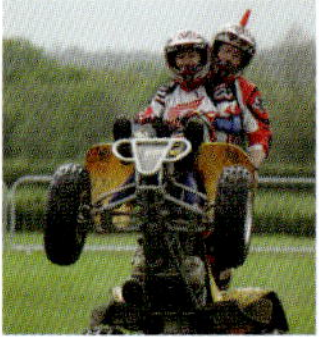
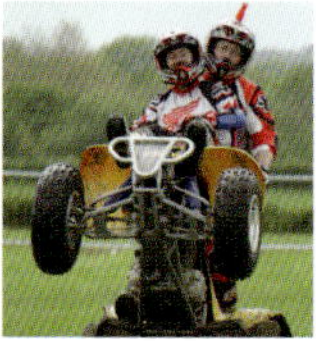
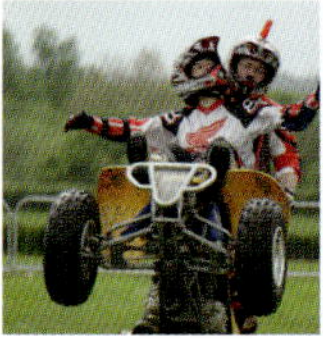

In this sequence of images, predictive AF has done a good job at keeping the subject in focus even though it is moving more or less toward the camera.

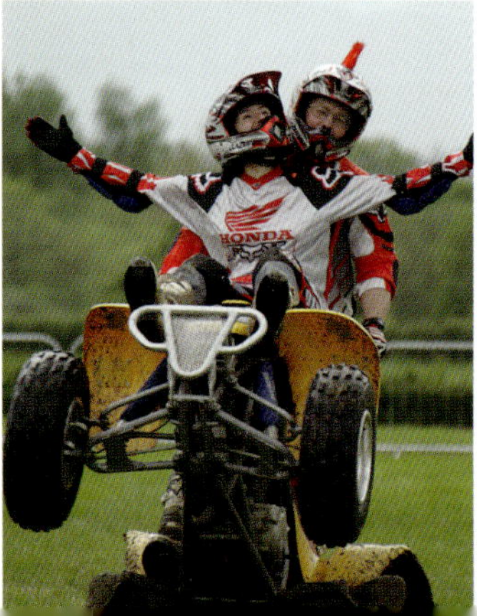

Manual focus

Although a DSLR camera's autofocus systems can cope in the majority of cases, there are a number of circumstances when you may need to switch to manual focus. If the subject exhibits little contrast, or is more or less the same color, the camera won't have enough "visual clues" to compare how the pixels contrast with one another at different focal ranges and therefore will be unable to find the optimum focusing distance. Alternatively there may be insufficient light for the camera to focus, especially if the subject is out of range of the autofocus lamp; while some photographers prefer to focus manually anyway. Whatever the reason, it pays to learn how to quickly switch your camera to focus manually; with many makes of camera, there's a manual override button on the lens or body, which makes the operation very quick. Check in your camera's manual if you're not sure how to switch to manual focus.

If you're shooting sports or action in which the subject only comes into view at the last minute, switch to manual focus and prefocus on the point where the subject will appear. When it moves into the viewfinder you can fire the shutter knowing the subject will be in focus.

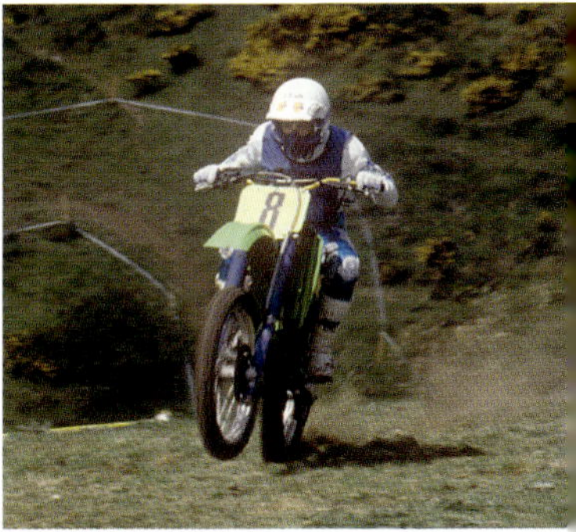

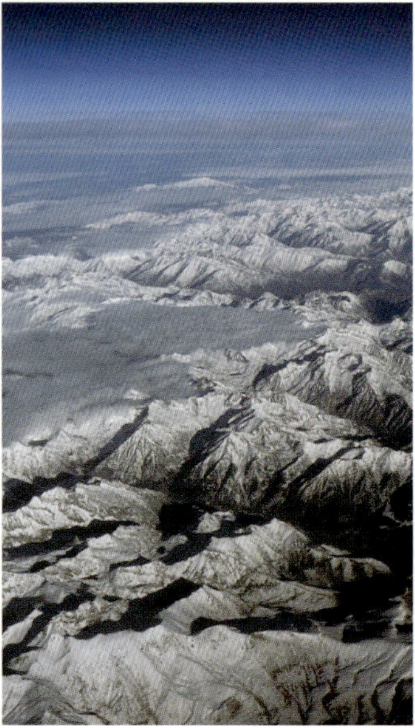

In subdued lighting, and particularly with low-contrast subjects, the camera's autofocus is likely to struggle. This is one of the most common circumstances when you will have to focus manually in order to get the shot.

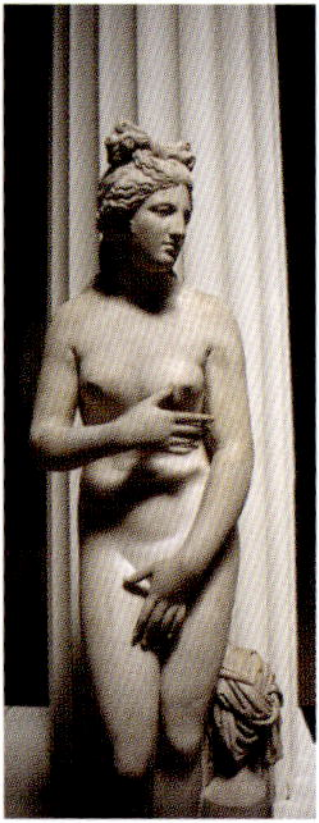

When confronted with certain types of glass, some cameras will try to focus on the glass rather than the scene behind the it. Flying in an airplane over the Pyrenees, here the photographer got as close to the window as possible, switched focus to manual, and took several shots of the spectacular scenery thousands of feet below him.

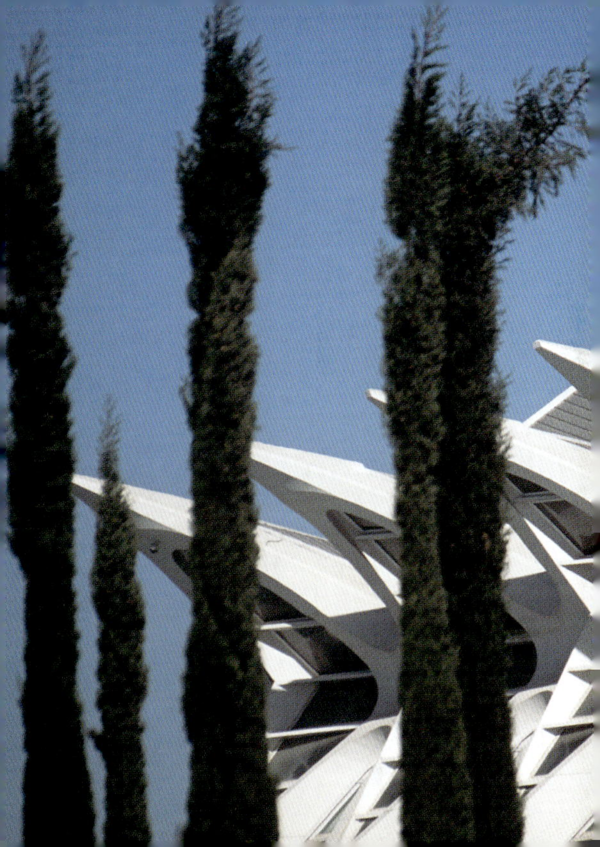

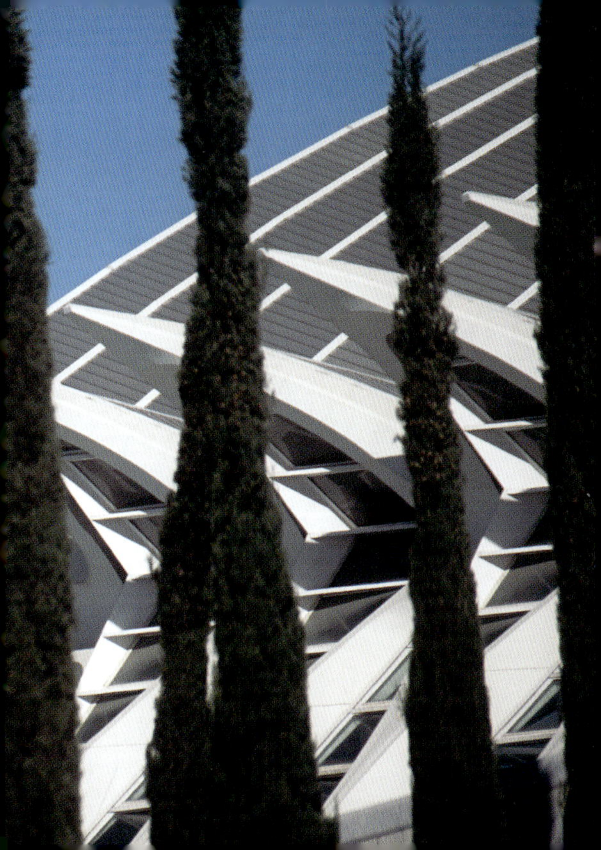

White Balance Presets

For those of you who are new to digital photography, any discussion of white balance may have your eyes glazing over. Essentially, white balance is concerned with the overall color of the light in which you're shooting. For example, light at the time of a dramatic sunset will have a distinctly reddish color cast to it, while interior lights, such as certain incandescent lights, can give off an orange glow. Our eyes are so good at adjusting for these color casts that we often aren't aware of them. But for a digital camera, unless the color of the lighting is addressed whites will not appear white, hence the term "white balance." In the case of the sunset, whites will appear rosy pink, while under incandescent light, white can appear orange.

Using the camera's Auto White Balance setting will usually provide pretty accurate results, and this is the best setting to leave the camera on. However, in extreme conditions you may need to turn to one of the white balance preset settings to get a more faithful-looking colors. Typical settings include Sunlight/Daylight; Cloudy/Twilight/Sunset; Shade; Incandescent/Tungsten; Fluorescent; Flash.

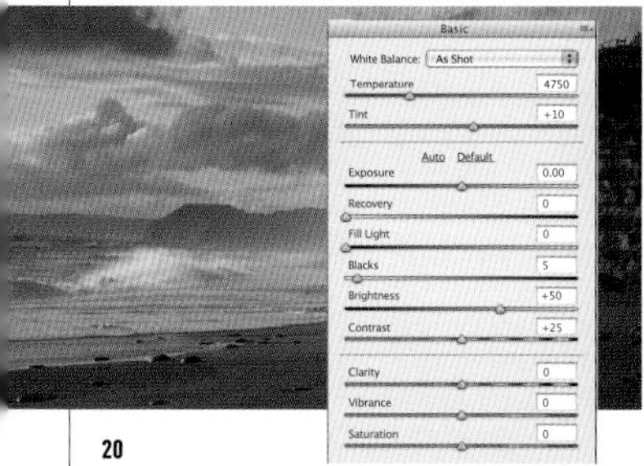

Shoot Raw

Remember if you shoot Raw you can choose whatever white balance setting you want at the time of taking the photo, and if you're not happy with your choice of setting adjust it later during post-production without losing any image quality whatsoever.

In the first image of stalactites, the incandescent light flooding the cave has produced a very unpleasant orange cast. Using the Incandescent white balance setting has produced a much more acceptable result, demonstrated by the white clothing.

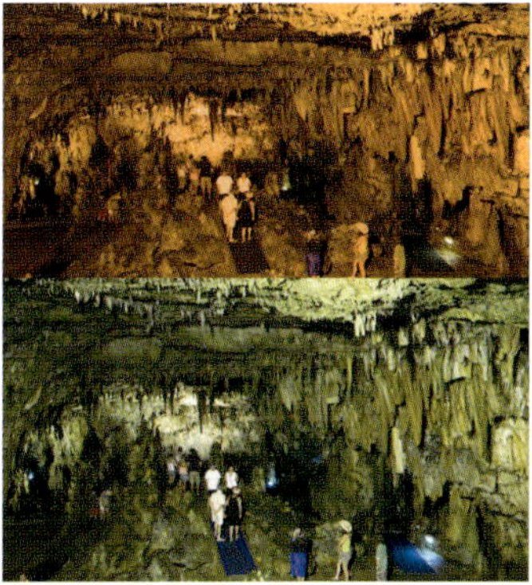

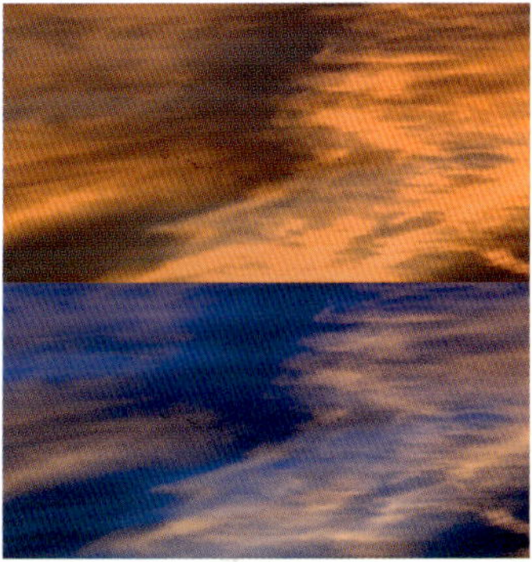

Getting rid of color casts is desirable in most cases. However, when shooting sunsets, adjusting the white balance setting so that you "correct" the orange glow may detract from the naturally emotive colors of a rich sunset.

Custom White Balance

Here's a quick and easy tip if achieving accurate white balance is important in difficult or mixed lighting situations. Select your camera's manual or custom white balance setting (most DSLRs now have one of these). Next, place a white object in front of the camera so that the camera can record how white will appear under the particular lighting conditions you're working in at that time. With some cameras it's simply a case of ensuring that the white object—a piece of white paper or card will suffice—fills a good element of the viewfinder (the spot circle for example), and then taking a shot. The camera will record the white balance setting, which will then become available as a custom preset in the white balance menu when you continue to photograph. With other cameras simply pressing a white balance button will record the white card and apply that setting to future shots. Check in your manual to see how your specific camera's custom white balance setting works. Some cameras work by recording a gray card, but the method is identical.

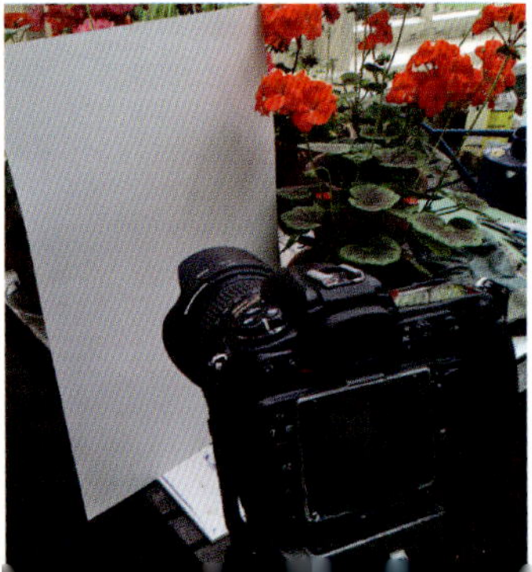

A camera being set up to record a custom white balance setting by taking a reading from a white card.

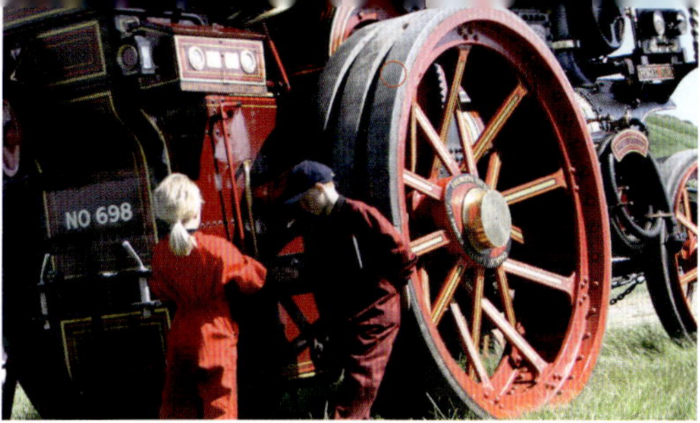

Look for gray reference

Most scenes will have at least one small area of neutral gray in them somewhere (here shown by the red circles). You can use this as a reference point as a way of getting fairly accurate white balance—particularly if it's not practical to shoot a white or gray card to set a custom white balance at the time of shooting. Make a mental note of the gray object or area, and when you edit the image in post-production you'll have a reference color to work to. Again, shooting in Raw will provide the best results if you need to adjust the color later.

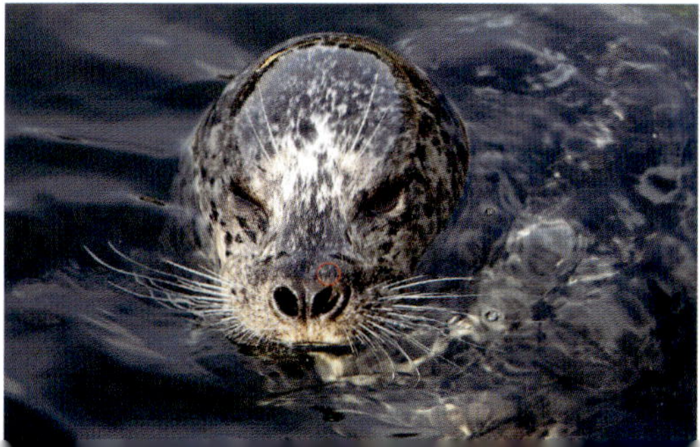

Shutter speed

In addition to having an impact on exposure, shutter speed can be used to alter how the subject appears within the image, in normal circumstances it is measured in fractions of a second.

Aperture values

Full stops	Half stops	Third stops
f/1.4	f/1.7	f/1.6 f/1.8
f/2	f/2.4	f/2.2 f/2.5
f/2.8	f/3.4	f/3.2 f/3.6
f/4	f/4.8	f/4.5 f/5
f/5.6	f/6.7	f/6.3 f/7.18
f/8	f/9.5	f/9 f/10
f/11	f/13	f/12 f/14
f/16	f/19	f/18 f/20
f/22		

The shutter speed is used to determine the length of an exposure in combination with the aperture value. If you increase the shutter speed, the aperture must be opened up wider to compensate. The scale used to measure the size of the aperture is known as the f/stop. It is the measurement of the diameter of the aperture plus the focal length of the lens. So with a zoom set to 40mm with an aperture of f/8 the diameter of the iris opening is 5mm (40 divided by 8). It is for this reason that an aperture of f/8 is smaller than f/4.

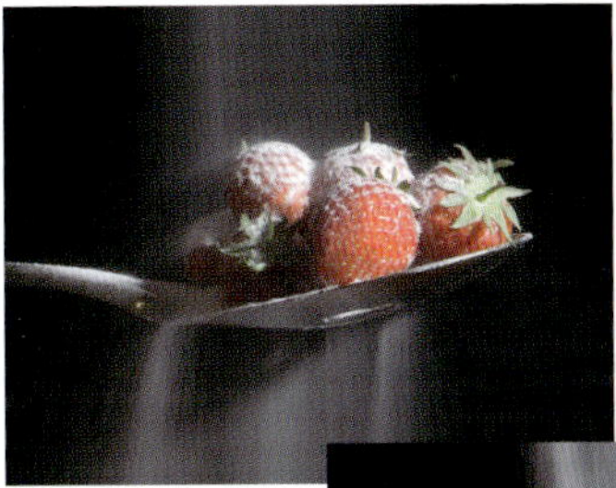

Slow 1/4 sec
Falling sugar has become a white haze.

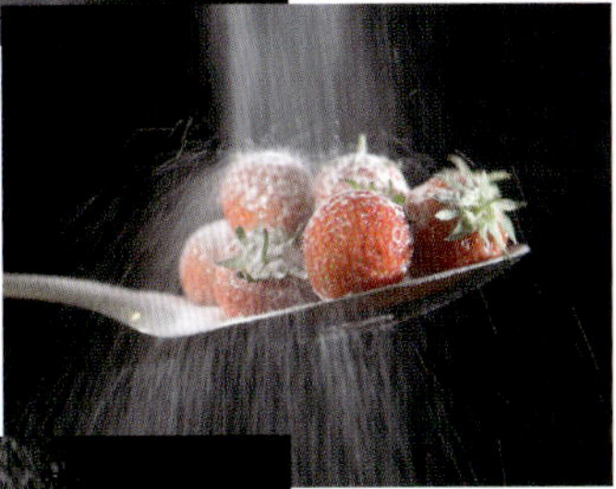

Medium 1/45 sec
Grains of sugar have become individual lines of white, tracing their route as they fall.

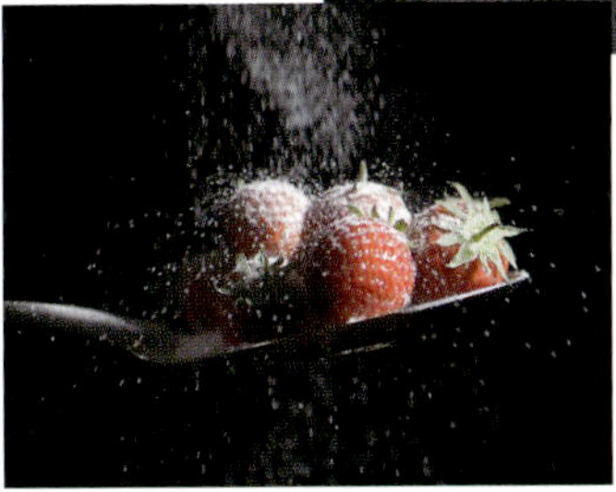

Fast 1/750 sec
The shutter speed allows some individual grains to be visible even though the movement is not frozen.

Avoiding camera shake

One of the most common causes of blurred pictures is camera shake. Camera shake occurs when the photographer uses a shutter speed that is slow enough to detect camera movement when the shutter release button is depressed. Ideally, for really sharp pictures, it's good practice to use a tripod and remote shutter release cable to keep the camera steady. However, this isn't always practical—few of us want to carry a tripod around with us wherever we go. Although there are no strict rules governing minimum shutter speeds for hand-held photography—some people are better at keeping the camera steady than others—there are guidelines. These are based on the effective focal length (efl) in use at the time of taking the photo. As a rule of thumb, you should make sure that the minimum shutter speed is a reciprocal of the effective focal length. For example, with a lens of effective focal length of 250mm, you should use a shutter speed of 1/250 sec or faster.

Minimum shutter speeds

This table provides a rough guide to the slowest advisable shutter speed when hand-holding the camera. The figures are only guidelines. Also consider:

- Some people can hold a camera more steadily than others, usually due to better technique (see page 28).
- Cold and windy conditions make it harder to hand-hold a camera.
- Camera shake is not a precise constant. Sometimes you might get away with slow shutter speeds, other times not.

Effective focal length	Minimum shutter speed
16mm	1/20 sec
28mm	1/30 sec
35mm	1/30 sec
80mm	1/90 sec
125mm	1/125 sec
200mm	1/250 sec
400mm	1/500 sec

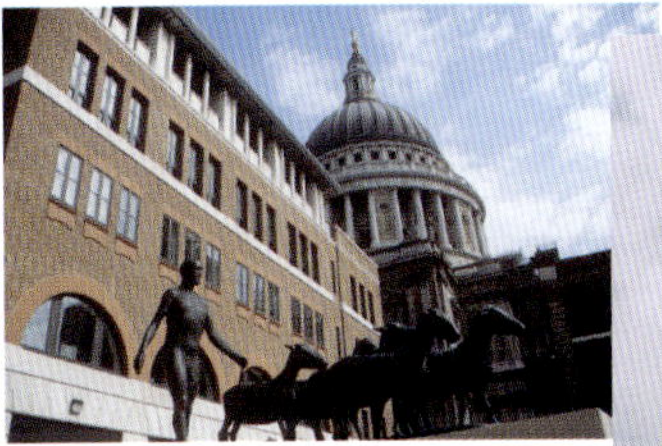

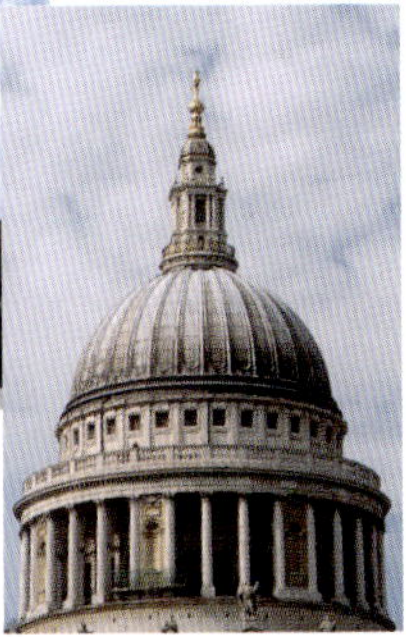

The likelihood of camera shake increases with focal length. The first shot of St Paul's Cathedral, London, was taken with a wide-angle lens of efl 20mm, and a relatively slow speed of 1/30 sec produced a sharp result. The second shot was taken with efl 250mm, and to avoid camera shake a shutter speed of 1/250 sec was used.

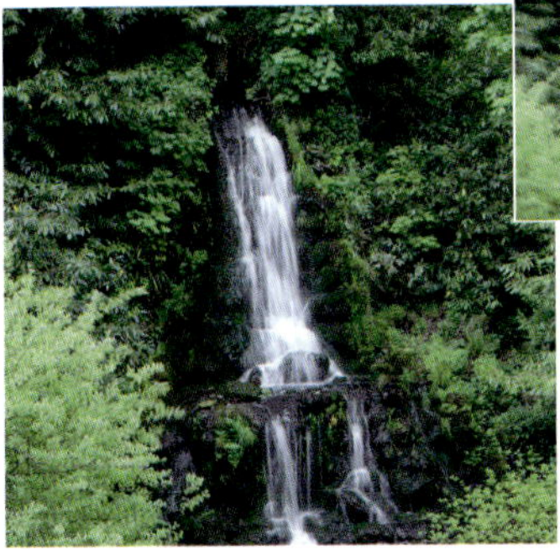

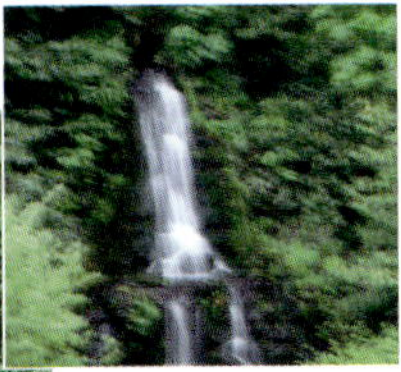

Shot in adverse weather, neither of these shots is tack sharp. However, the first is acceptable, given the circumstances and the 1/10 sec shutter speed. The second is so blurred that it is entirely unusable.

How to stay steady

Even if you follow the guidelines outlined in the previous pages regarding shutter speed and focal length, you'll further improve your chances of capturing sharp images if you learn a few basic techniques. The most important is how to hold the camera. Begin with a firm base. Stand with your feet around shoulder width apart, with one foot slightly in front of the other. Hold the camera grip firmly in your right hand, and support the bottom of the lens in your left hand. This will also let you adjust the focus and zoom rings on the len's barrel. Finally, keep your elbows comfortably tucked into your body. When it comes to taking the shot, don't hold your breath. Keep breathing gently, and squeeze the shutter release just after you exhale.

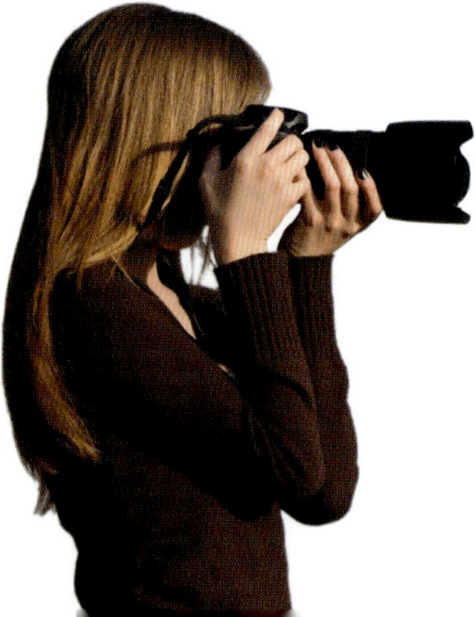

Image stabilization

Image stabilization, or vibration reduction as it is also known, is the name given to a number of ways in which digital cameras reduce the effect of camera-shake when using slow shutter speeds during hand-held shooting. There are two main types of image stabilization. The first involves sensors in the lens that detect and measure movement. The sensors relay this information to the optical elements, which in turn move accordingly, making minute adjustments so that the image being focused on the sensor allows for any camera shake thereby producing as sharp an image as possible.

The second system works in a similar way, but instead of locating the sensors in the lens, the sensors are located in the camera. When they detect movement, the camera's main imaging sensor is adjusted by tiny servo motors, again to ensure the image remains as sharp as possible. Both systems work extremely well, allowing the photographer to obtain sharp images using shutter speeds that are two or even three stops slower than would normally be possible. This means that it becomes possible to use a 500mm lens with shutter speeds of 1/125 sec or even 1/60 sec.

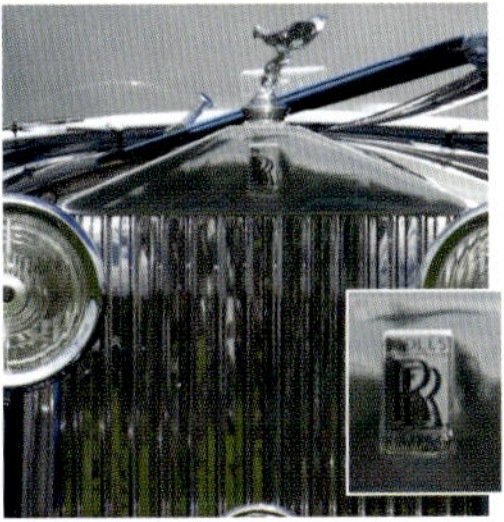

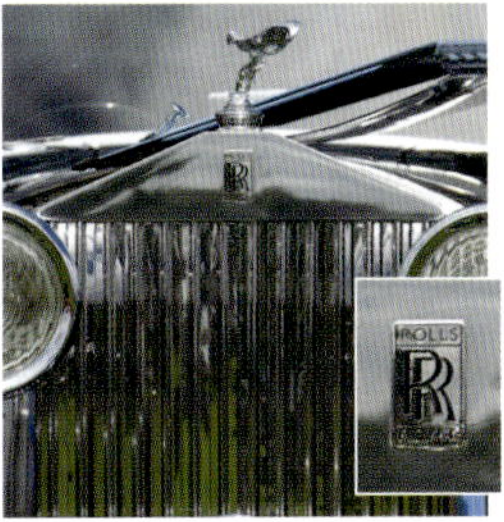

Image stabilization is particularly helpful when using longer telephoto lenses. These shots of a classic car were taken using an efl of 450mm at a shutter speed of 1/250 sec. The inset detail right reveals how an image stabilization system is able to produce a much sharper shot.

Freezing motion

When it comes to photographing action, such as sports, our natural inclination is to use shutter speeds that are fast enough to freeze the action. Such shots reveal and allow us to examine detail—the expression on a golfer's face as he is about to strike the ball, for example—that we wouldn't have time to consider when watching in real time with the naked eye. Exactly how fast the shutter speed needs to be depends on several factors; how fast the subject is moving; the distance between the subject and the camera; the effective focal length; and the direction the subject is moving in relation to the camera.

Minimum shutter speeds for freezing action

Subject	Speed	Distance	Focal length	Direction of movement		
				Across frame	Toward camera	Diagonal
Car	50mph (80km/h)	30m	100mm	1/1000 sec	1/250 sec	1/125 sec
Car	100mph (160km/h)	30m	100mm	1/2000 sec	1/500 sec	1/1000 sec
Sprinter	12mph (20km/h)	10m	200mm	1/1500 sec	1/350 sec	1/750 sec
Sprinter	12mph (20km/h)	20m	300mm	1/1000 sec	1/250 sec	1/500 sec
Train	100mph (160km/h)	50m	35mm	1/500 sec	1/125 sec	1/250 sec
Train	100mph (160km/h)	50m	200mm	1/3000 sec	1/750 sec	1/1500 sec
Jogger	6mph (10km/h)	5m	100mm	1/750 sec	1/180 sec	1/300 sec
Jogger	6mph (10km/h)	2m	35mm	1/750 sec	1/180 sec	1/300 sec
Jet plane	500mph (800km/h)	2000m	400mm	1/500 sec	1/125 sec	1/250 sec
Jet plane	500mph (800km/h)	1000m	400mm	1/1000 sec	1/250 sec	1/500 sec

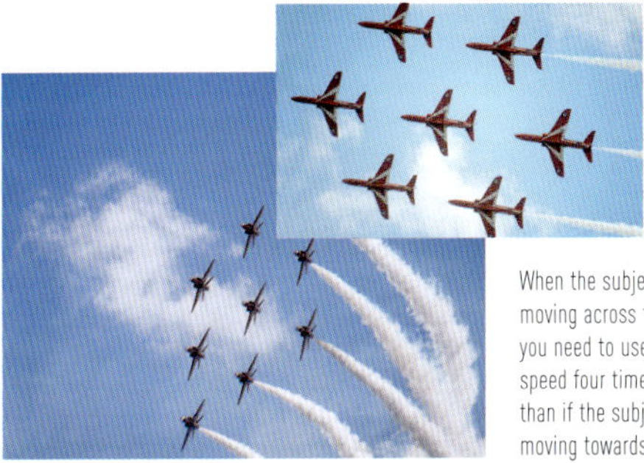

When the subject is moving across the frame, you need to use a shutter speed four times faster than if the subject was moving towards you.

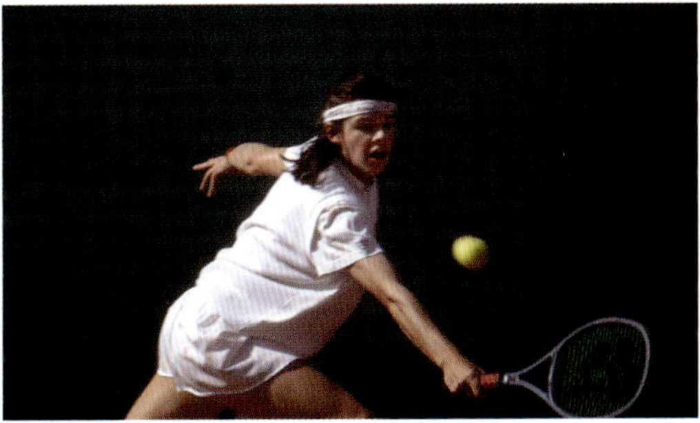

Not all parts of a moving subject are necessarily moving at the same speed or in the same direction. Here the player herself has been frozen, but the ball, which is moving faster and across the frame, is still slightly blurred—in this example adding to the sense of action.

Creative blurring

Freezing the action seems an intuitive way to capture movement. Images are crisp, detail is easily identifiable, and the specific "moment in time" is clear for everyone to see. However, this commonly used technique can lead to images that appear to lack dynamism—as one photographer put it, with very fast shutter speeds it's hard to distinguish between a racing car that's hurtling around the track at 200 mph (320 km/h) and one that's stationary.

One way to reintroduce a sense of movement is to deliberately use a relatively slow shutter speed, so that the subject, or at least its fastest moving elements, are blurred. This recreates more accurately what our brain perceives, adds life and energy to the image, and generally makes it more realistic. Exactly what shutter speed to use to get the right effect is often a case of trial and error.

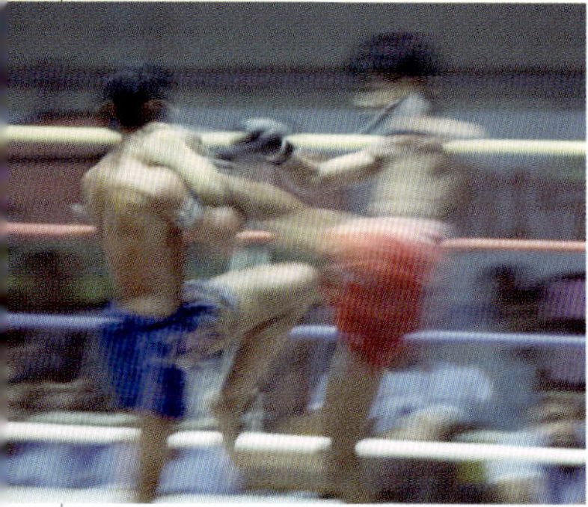

Using a shutter speed of 1/30 sec has resulted in this image of Thai kick boxers becoming a blur of arms and legs. This helps to convey the incredible speed at which they're moving.

Panning

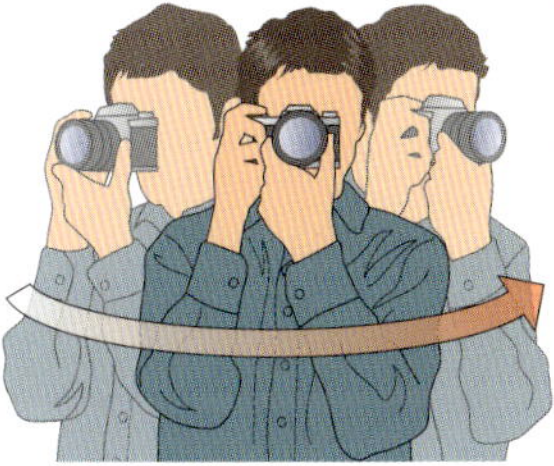

As well as experimenting with slower shutter speeds, try following the subject in the viewfinder as it moves passed you, releasing the shutter when it is directly in front of you. This technique is called panning. The idea is to freeze the majority of the subject, while rendering the background a streaky blur.

- Hold the camera as you do normally, with your feet slightly apart.
- Track the subject as it comes into view from one side by swinging your shoulders and turning on your hips. The whole upper part of your body will swing through around 90°.
- Focus as quickly as you can once you get the subject in the viewfinder. Keep tracking the subject, and gently squeeze the release as it moves in front of you. Use a shutter speed of between 4–16 times longer than you would if you were attempting to freeze the action, and try shooting in continuous mode to get lots of frames.
- Keep tracking the subject even after it's passed and you've taken your finger off the shutter release.
- Keep practising the technique and you'll find you get more proficient with time.

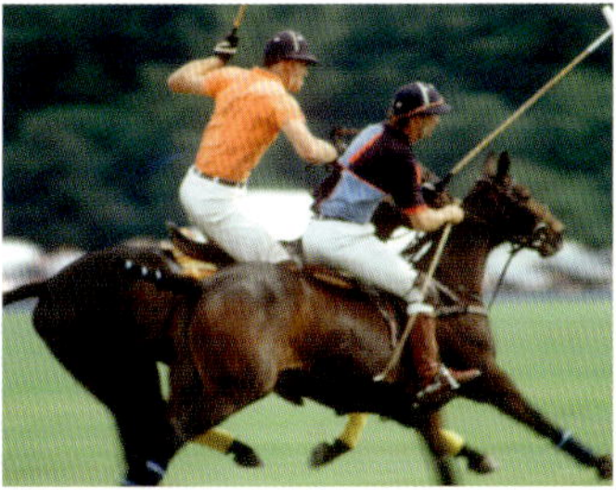

If done well, panning can have two effects. First, it conveys a sense of movement, and second, by blurring the background it becomes less of a distraction to the viewer.

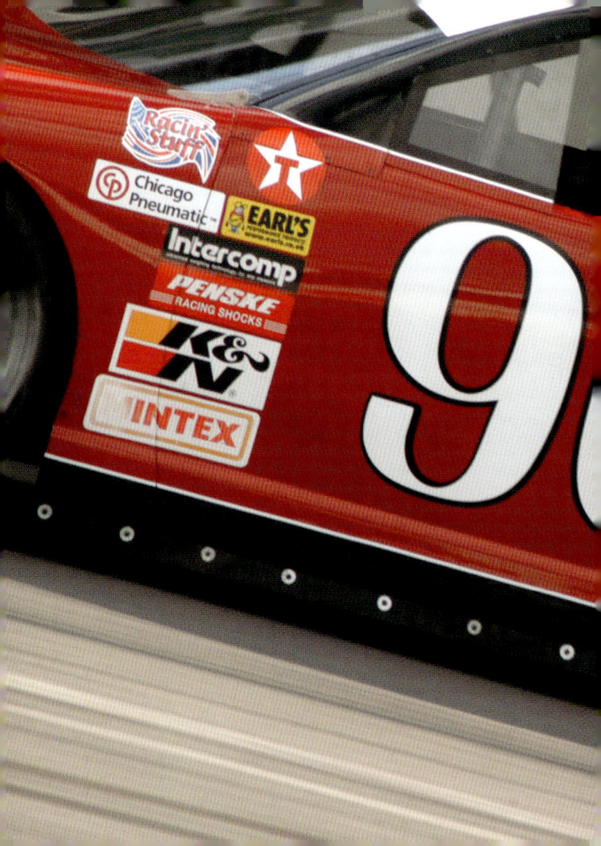
Racin' Stuff
Chicago Pneumatic
EARL'S
Intercomp
PENSKE
RACING SHOCKS
K&N
INTEX
9

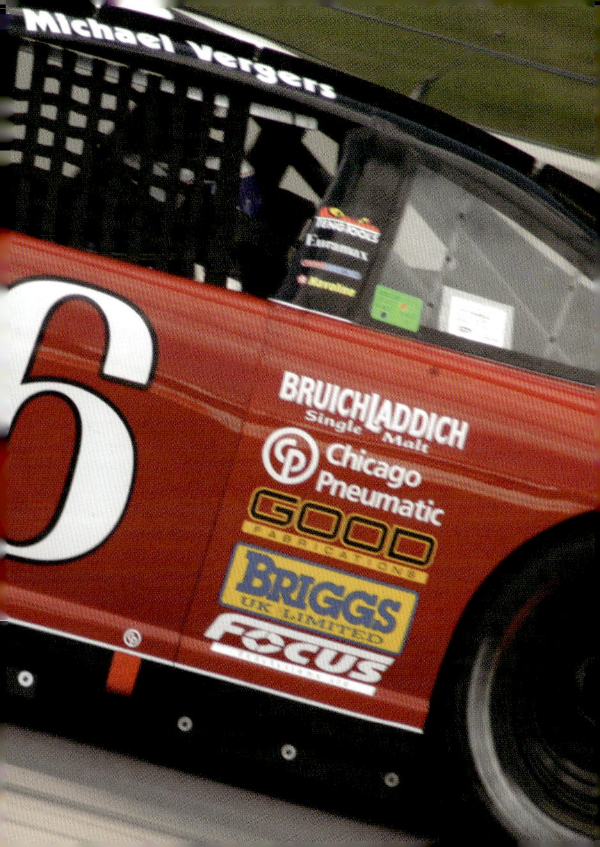
Michael Vergers
6
BRUICHLADDICH
Single Malt
Chicago
Pneumatic
GOOD
FABRICATIONS
BRIGGS
UK LIMITED
FOCUS

Understanding depth of field

The term depth of field refers to the extent of the area in front of the camera in which objects appear in focus. It is one of the most creative weapons a photographer has in his or her armory. Depth of field is controlled primarily by the aperture setting. A wide aperture setting (small number) results in a narrow depth of field, while a small aperture setting (large number) will provide a greater depth of field. But other factors also come into play. A short focal length setting has a wider depth of field than a long focal length setting. In other words, a wide-angle lens will keep more of a scene in focus than a telephoto lens. Another factor is how far the subject is from the camera. The nearer it is to the camera, the narrower the depth of field.

Varying focal length

These two shots show how depth of field increases with shorter focal length. The aperture was set to f/5.6 and the point of focus was the green pepper. The camera was moved closer to the peppers to achieve similar pictures.

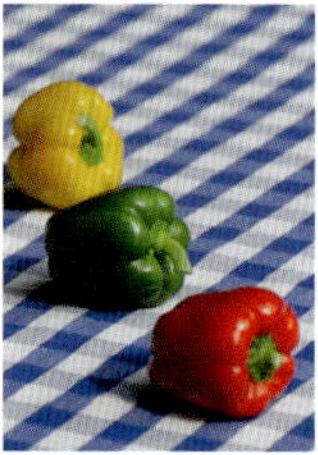

135MM

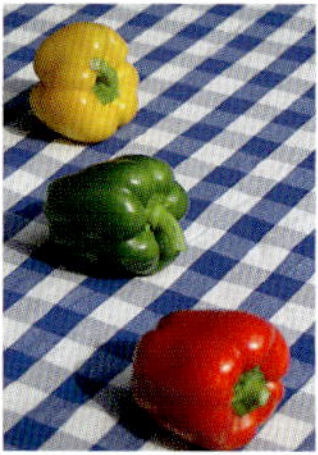

45MM

In the left-hand image, the longer focal length (135mm) has rendered the red and yellow peppers out of focus. Notice also how the image is foreshortened. In the right-hand image, the shorter focal length (45mm) has resulted in all the peppers being noticeably sharper.

Varying aperture

The three shots below were all taken with efl 80mm. The point of focus was the top of the middle pepper.

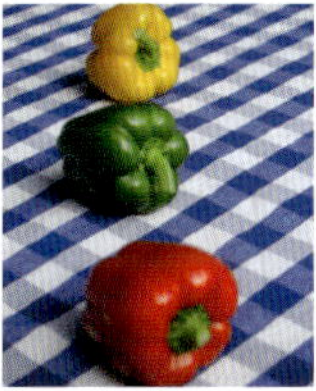

f/4.5: The widest aperture setting provides the narrowest depth of field.

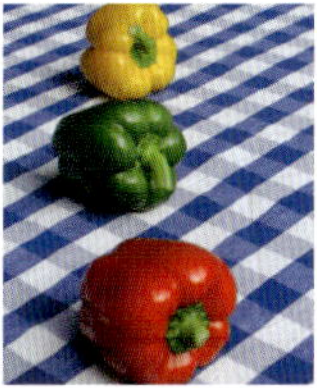

f/8: A mid-aperture setting increases depth of field.

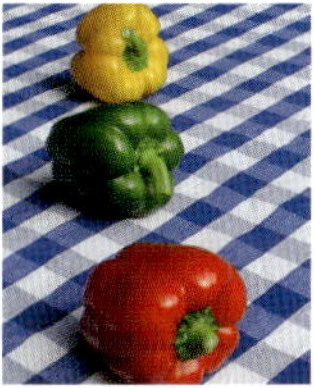

f/16: The smallest aperture setting provides the greatest depth of field

Varying focused distance

The three shots were taken with the same efl 80mm and f/11 setting. The point of focus was changed.

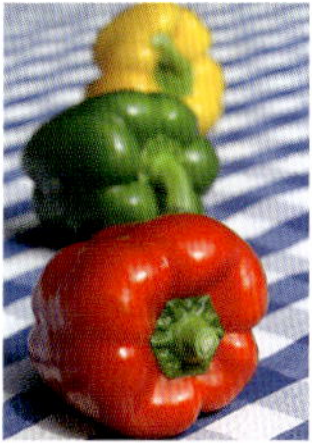

Focusing on the first pepper provides least depth of field.

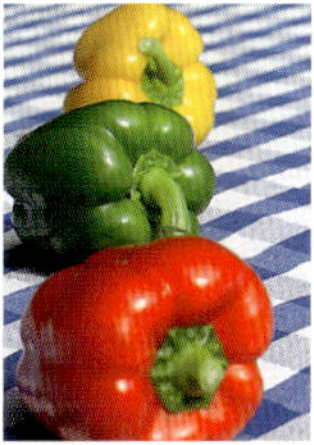

Focus is on the middle pepper.

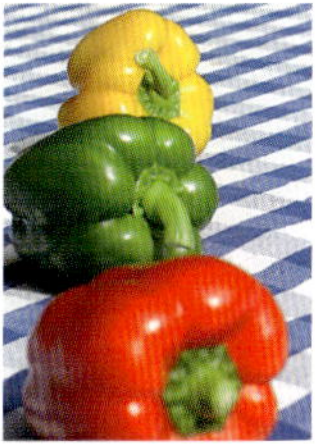

Focusing on the far pepper provides greatest depth.

Maximizing depth of field

In certain types of shots, such as a traditional landscape, for example, your aim will be to get as much of the image in focus as possible. To maximize depth of field use a wide-angle lens (or the widest focal length setting on a zoom), shoot so that any foreground objects are as far away from the camera as possible, and, finally, choose the narrowest aperture (highest number) that you can. Remember a small aperture setting may mean you have to use a slow shutter speed, so watch out for camera shake. Use a tripod or a steady surface if this is likely, or increase the ISO setting.

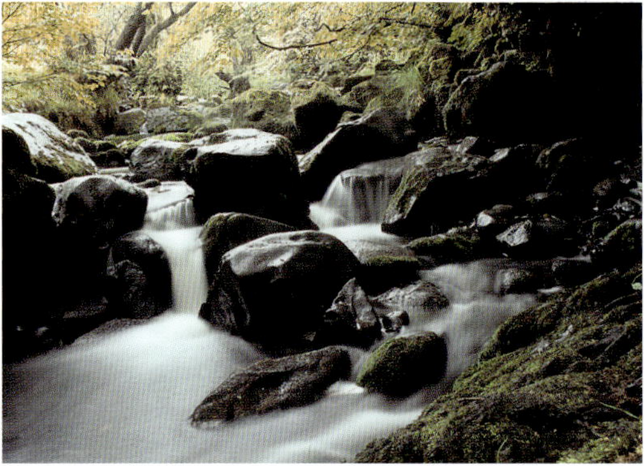

Using efl 20mm and an aperture setting of f/22 helped to keep everything from near foreground to the trees in the background, in focus in this woodland scene. The relatively dark lighting and the small aperture resulted in a lengthy exposure of 30 sec, turning the moving water to a soft foam.

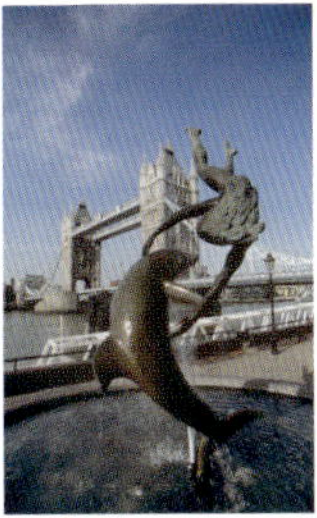

An ultra-wide angle 18mm lens ensured everything was in focus in this London scene.

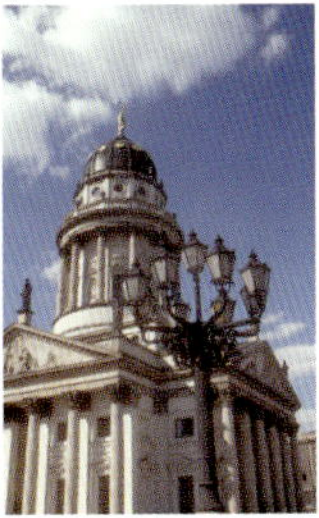

Including something in the foreground helps to add depth to an image.

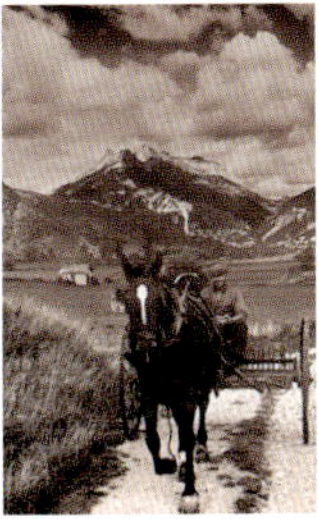

Bright conditions allowed for a small aperture in this shot of a French farmer.

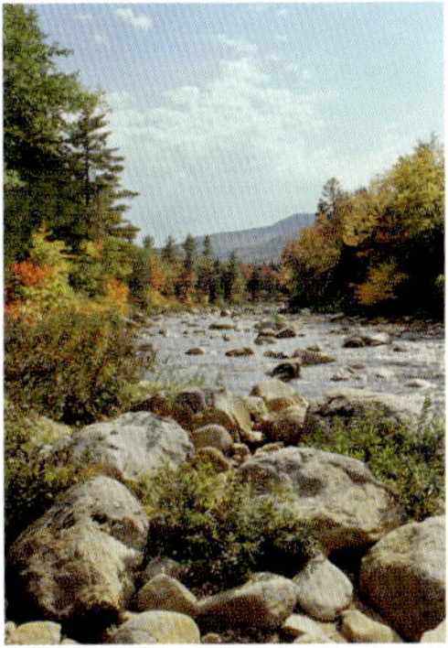

Hyperfocal distance

To obtain maximum depth of field, use a wide-angle focal length and switch to manual focus. Instead of focusing on the main subject of your scene, focus just beyond the closest element that you want to appear in focus in the composition. With luck this will be the hyperfocal distance, the point of focus where everything from half that distance to infinity will be sharp. Because modern cameras rarely have depth-of-field scales on the lenses anymore, it's not possible to work out the hyperfocal distance with any certainty, but with a little trial and error you should be able to increase depth.

Minimizing depth of field

If you're used to a point-and-shoot camera, which, due to their small sensors and short focal length lenses, tend to have a very wide depth of field, it might seem a bit strange to actually want to restrict depth of field. But being able to deliberately create a narrow zone of sharpness is one of the most creative aspects of photography. When you selectively focus on the subject, deliberately ensuring the background and/or foreground are out of focus, the viewer's eye is instantly drawn to the isolated subject, and, because it's not how our eyes normally register a scene, there is an added impact to the shot.

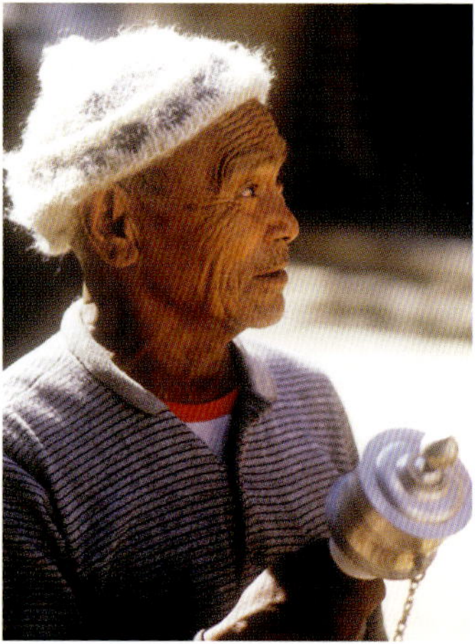

Portraits are an excellent subject in which to restrict depth of field. Using a wide aperture and long focal length helps to isolate the subject from a potentially distracting background.

How to restrict depth of field

There are three key ways in which you can easily minimize depth of field:

- Choose as wide an aperture setting as possible, while still ensuring you're obtaining good exposure.
- Use a telephoto lens or long focal length setting.
- Get as close to the subject as possible. Depth of field decreases the closer the lens is focused.

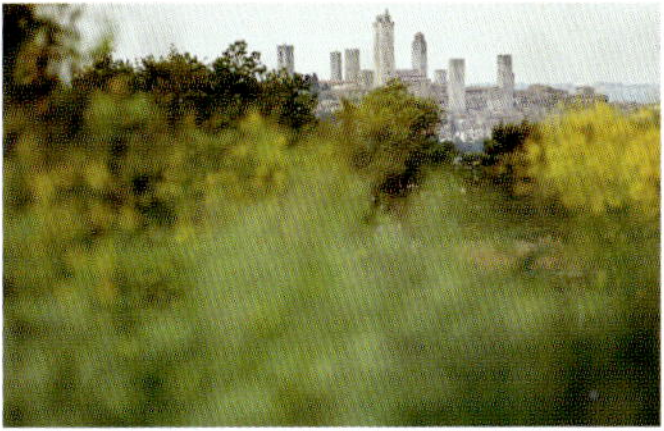

Narrow depth of field is equally effective at blurring unwanted foregrounds as well as backgrounds.

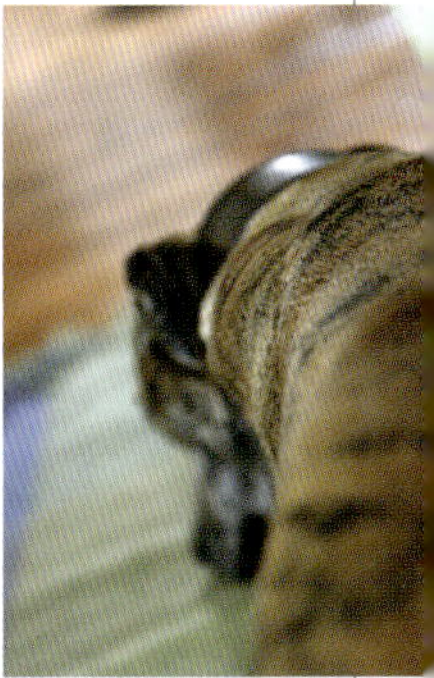

Getting as close as possible to your subject and selecting a wide aperture setting will restrict you to a very narrow depth of field.

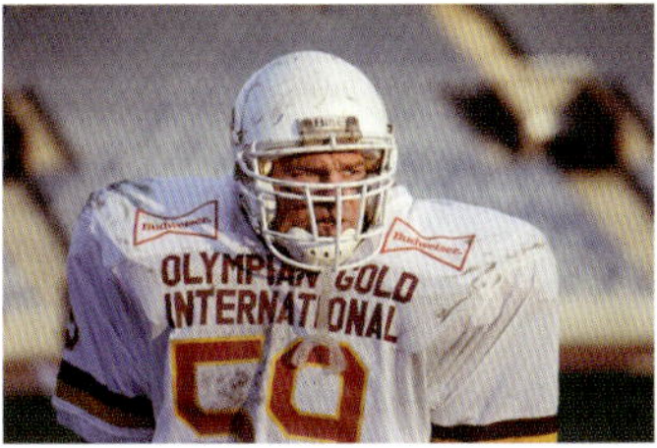

Minimizing depth of field with certain sports photography can help to blur advertising hoardings and spectators. Most sports photography is shot with long telephoto lenses, which helps to isolate the subject.

"Stop down" for quality

Because of the way they are constructed, lenses will usually provide sharper images at certain aperture settings. At very wide apertures, spherical aberration (in which the rays of light don't all focus accurately to create a perfect focal point) will cause the image to blur, particularly at the edges. As you "stop down" (reduce the size of the aperture) image quality will improve as spherical aberration becomes less of an issue. Continue to stop down, however, and again quality falls off. This is because the light diffracts as it passes through the very narrow aperture—again resulting in a softer image.

Therefore, if the conditions you're shooting under, combined with the result you're trying to achieve, don't necessitate having to use the widest or narrowest aperture setting then don't; use a mid-sized aperture. Which is the best will depend on your particular lens, but f/8 and f/11 are often regarded as "sweet spots" with standard quality lenses. Set up a controlled test using a tripod, shoot the same scene through each aperture setting, and examine the results at 100 percent on your monitor, paying close attention to the edges of each shot.

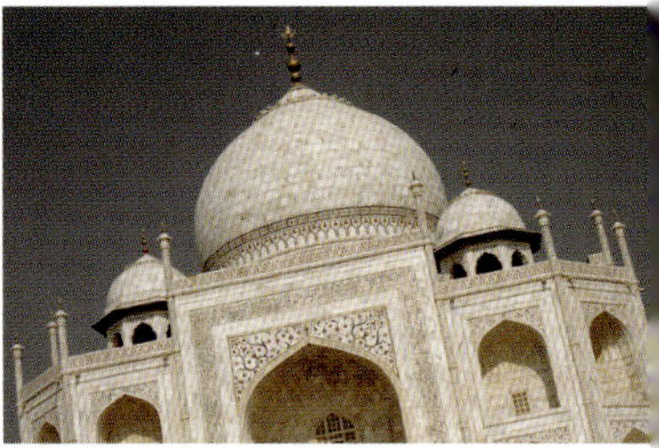

The bright conditions and relatively flat subject being shot some distance away allowed the photographer to use a mid-sized aperture to maximize resolution.

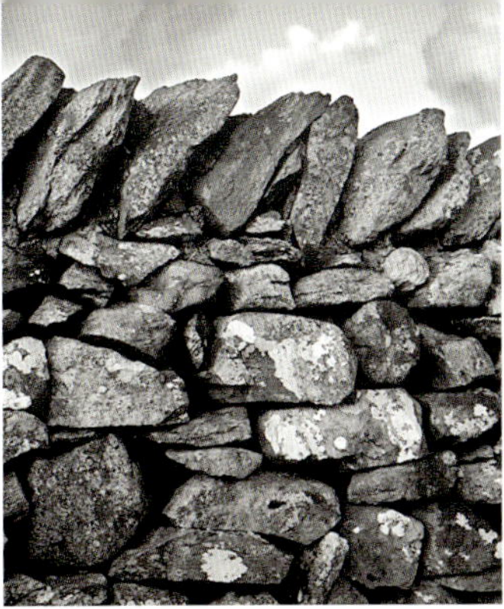

When the subject is more or less parallel to the camera, such as this drystone wall, having a wide depth of field is not a consideration, so an aperture of f/8 was used.

The depth of field was not important in this telephoto shot of a goat at an agricultural show, the an aperture setting of f/8 was used to capture as much detail in the animal's coat as possible.

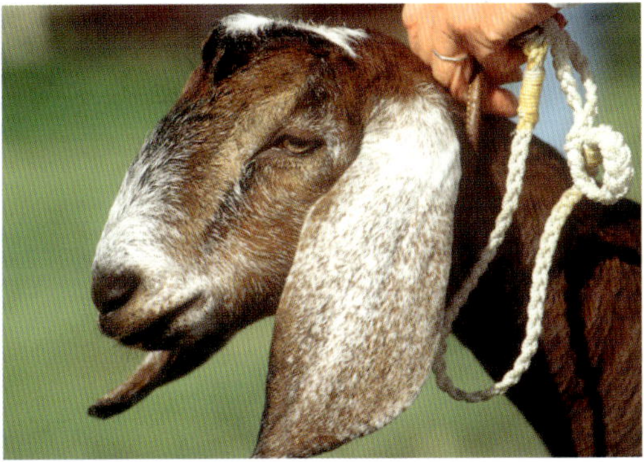

Manipulate the background

Changing focal length alters the angle of view. For example, use a telephoto lens to take a head-and-shoulders portrait, then recreate a similar head-and-shoulders portrait using a wide-angle lens—obviously you'll have to get much closer to the subject. Now compare the two shots. Although the portraits will look similar, if you compare the backgrounds you'll see they differ drastically. In this way you can manipulate backgrounds by experimenting with different focal lengths.

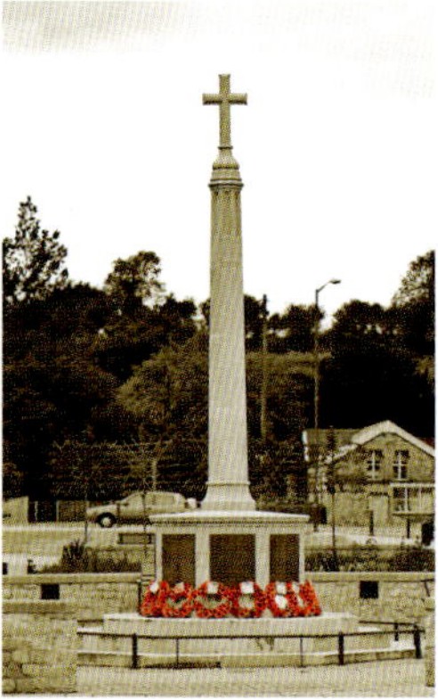

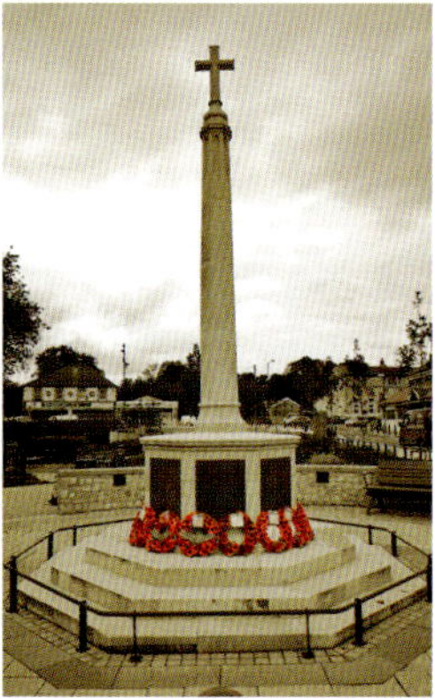

Compare these two shots of a war memorial. The one on the left was taken with a telephoto lens, the one on the right with a wide-angle lens from a much closer position. The difference in the angle of view renders the two backgrounds almost unrecognizable.

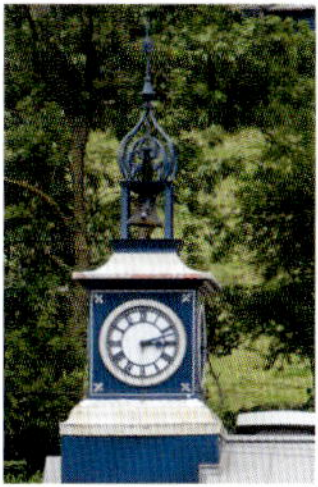

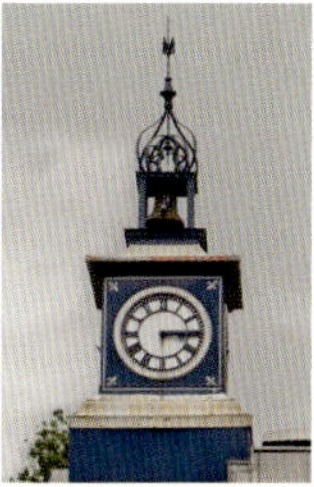

By moving further away from the subject you can alter the background. From close-up, the clock tower is pictured in front of a cloudy sky; from further back with a longer lens, trees and the roof of another building provide a background that adds greater context.

Even with the subject placed close to the background, the amount of background visible varies significantly when focal length and subject distance are altered.

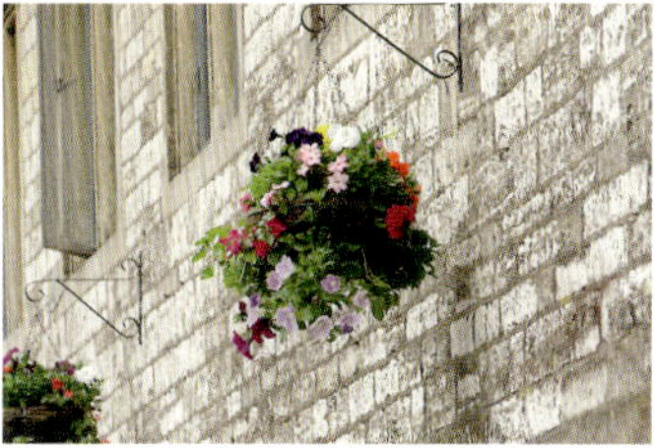

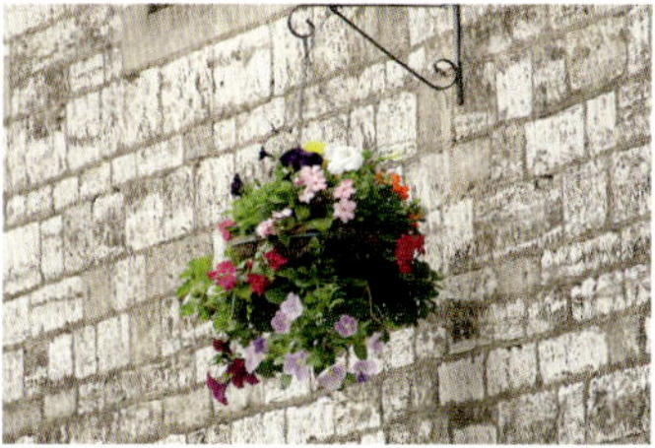

Using wide-angle lenses

Any lens with an effective focal length of 35mm or less is said to be wide-angle. The benefit of wide-angle lenses is that they offer a greater field of view, allowing you to capture more of the scene in front of the camera. The shorter the focal length, the greater the amount of scene that comes into view. Photographers can exploit a wider-angle of view in a number of ways.

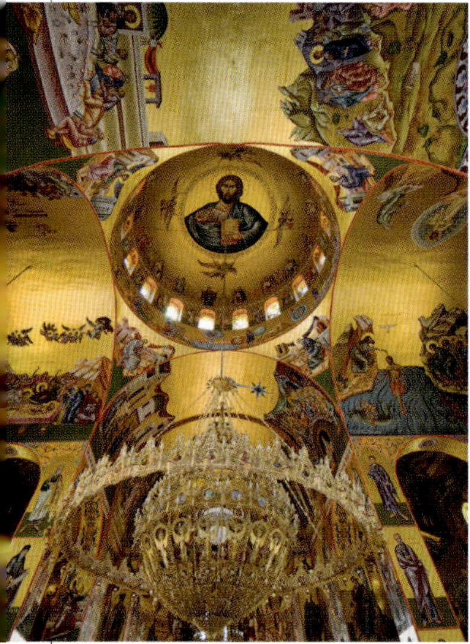

One of the most common uses of wide-angle lenses is for shooting interiors and other forms of architecture. This shot of the extraordinary murals found in a cathedral in Kefalonia would not have been possible with a standard focal length lens.

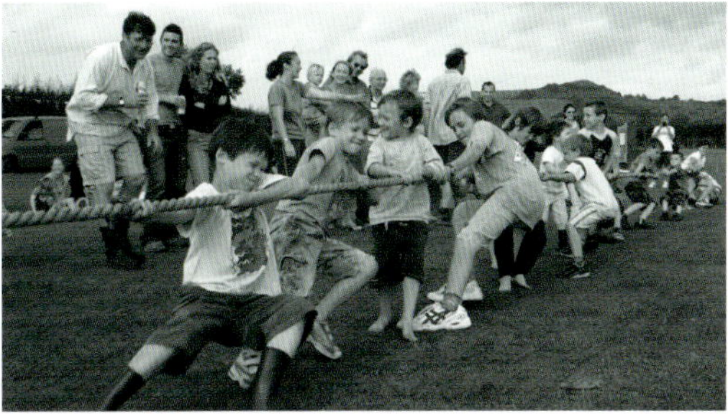

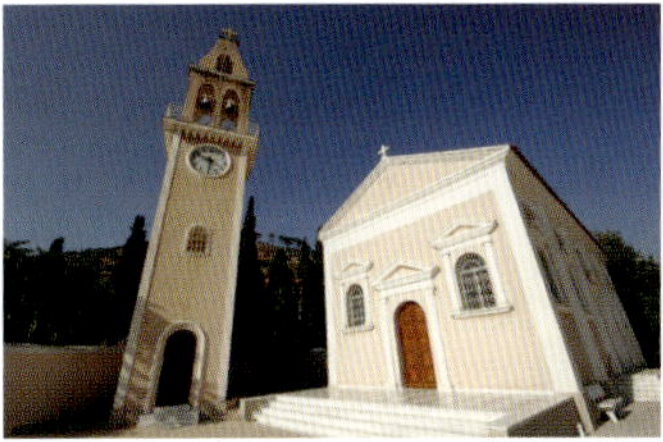

Wide-angle lenses have greater depth of field than other lenses, which can be exploited for good compositional use.

Wide-angle lenses complement sweeping landscapes, but need to have foreground interest.

Shot with an ultra wide-angle efl of 16mm, one of the side-products of such short focal lengths is exaggerated converging verticals, which occur when a lens is pointed upwards at buildings.

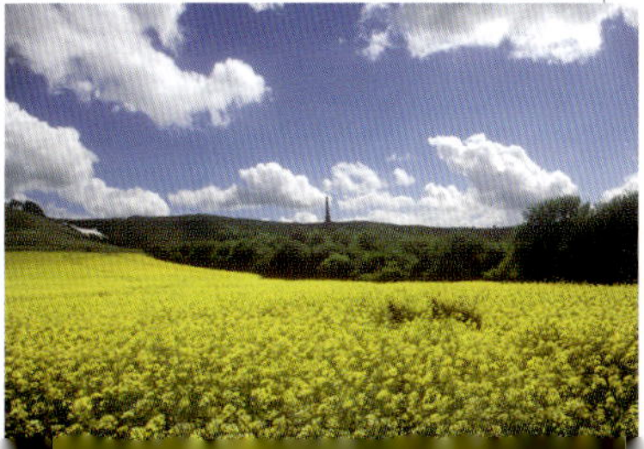

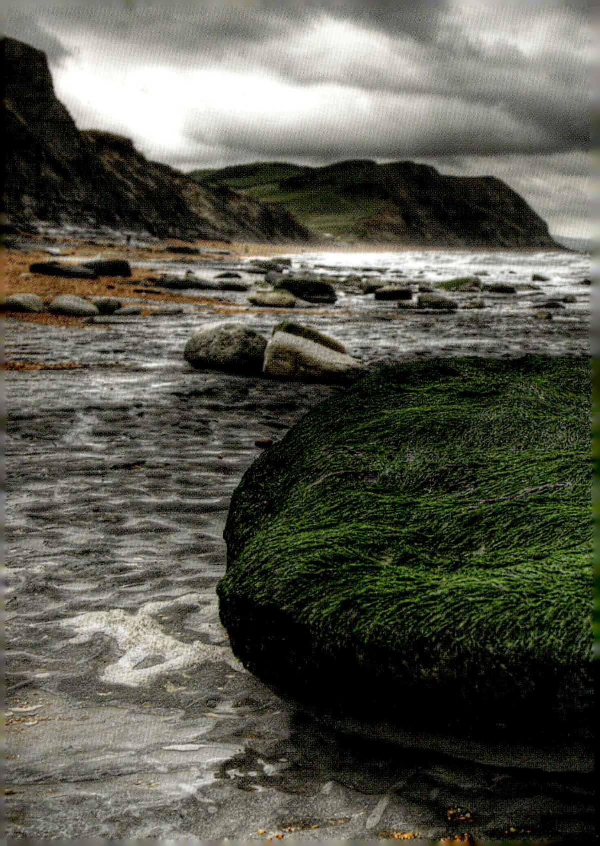

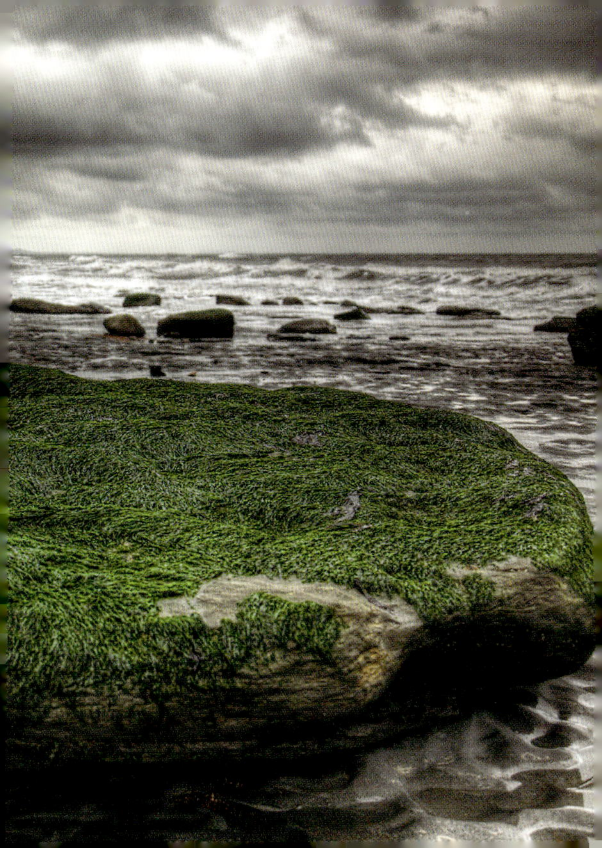

Using telephotos

Any lens that has a narrower angle of view than that perceived by human vision is said to be a telephoto lens. Such lenses can have an effective focal length of 70mm or more, with 800mm lenses (efl 1200mm on cropped-sensor cameras) having the maximum practical focal length. The main purpose of a telephoto lens is to magnify distant subjects so that they fill an appreciable portion of the frame. While such lenses are used primarily to shoot wildlife, sports, and news images, their optical properties can also be put to good use in landscape and portrait photography.

Although telephoto lenses aren't often naturally associated with landscape photography, this sunset image of rolling countryside shows how the short telephoto efl 105mm helps to foreshorten the view so helping to create the horizontal layered effect.

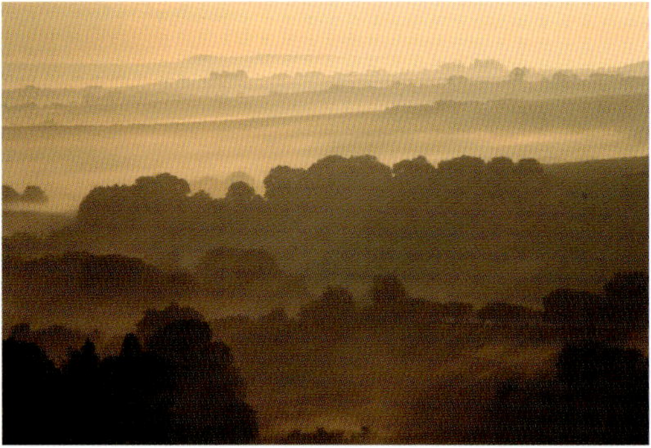

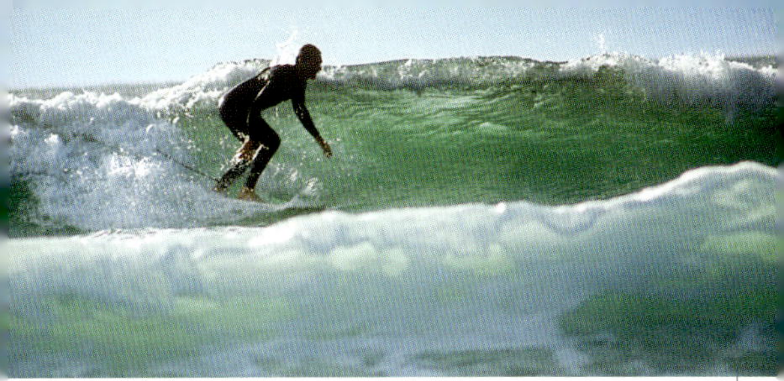

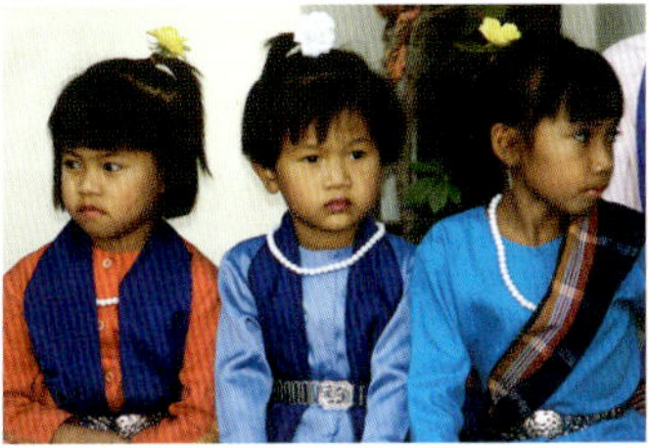

Telephoto lenses get you closer to the action. This surfer shot was taken from shallow water using a 400mm prime lens that provided an efl of 600mm on a cropped-sensor camera.

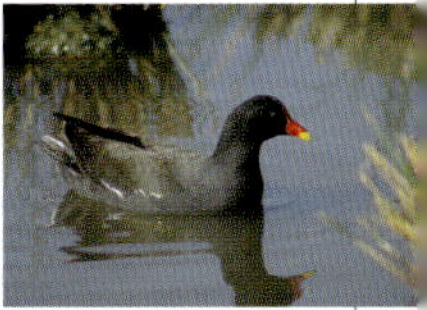

Short telephotos are the lenses of choice for portraits because they provide a slightly compressed perspective that flatters by slightly flattening facial features. Longer telephoto lenses come into their own for candid shots, such as this image which was taken with efl 300mm.

The smaller the bird and the more timid its behavior, the longer the lens needs to be. This shot was taken with a zoom lens offering an efl of 450mm.

Reading histograms

The ability to interpret histograms will help you to differentiate between poorly exposed shots and those that have a good tonal range. A histogram is simply a visual representation of how tones are distributed in an image. It analyzes the brightness value of each pixel on a scale from 0–255, with 0 (on the left) being pure black, and 255 (on the right) being bright white. The histogram shows this information in the form of a bar graph, showing how many pixels of each brightness value is contained in the image.

It is the shape and overall position of the histogram that really counts. If too much of the histogram is bunched up to the left, then the image is likely to be underexposed, if bunched to the right, overexposure is likely to be an issue. And if a lot of pixels are pushed up against either end then you have real problems. A tower of pixels running along the left edge indicates all the shadow regions have filled in and lost detail, while pixels running along the right-hand edge tell you that you have a large area of "blown" highlights in the shot, such as an overexposed sky that is completely white and devoid of any detail.

Anatomy of a histogram

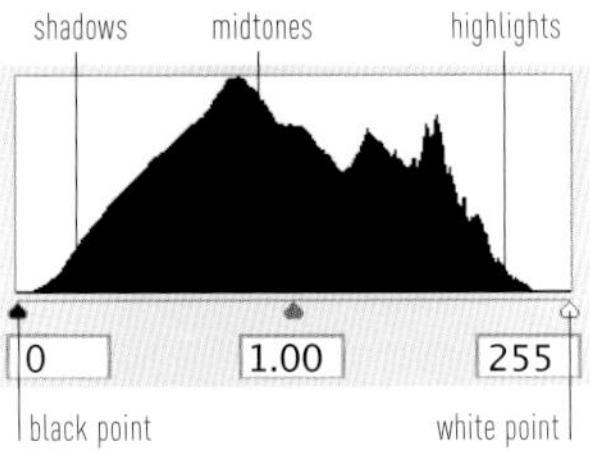

This histogram indicates a shot with a good spread of tonal values with no blown highlights or filled-in shadow regions. It's important to remember, however, if you're shooting Raw, the histogram displayed by the camera is that of a processed JPEG so doesn't necessarily represent the tonal values of your Raw data entirely accurately.

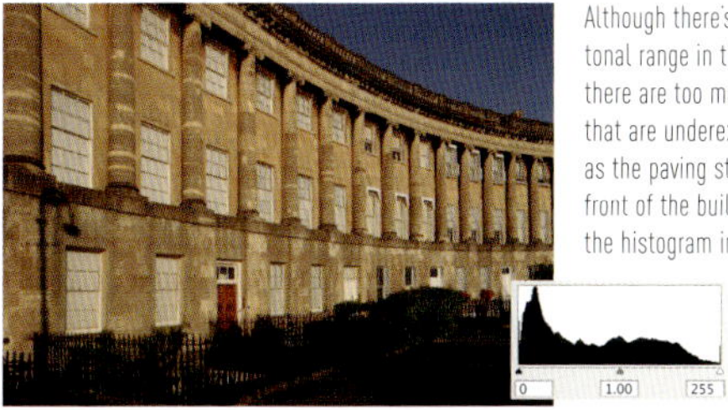

Although there's fairly wide tonal range in this image, there are too many areas that are underexposed, such as the paving stones at the front of the buildings, as the histogram indicates.

Again there is good tonal range in this shot, but the spike of pixels pushed up against the white point warns of blown highlights.

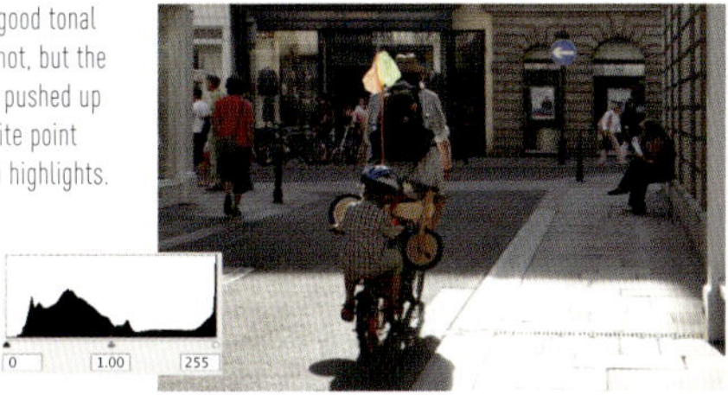

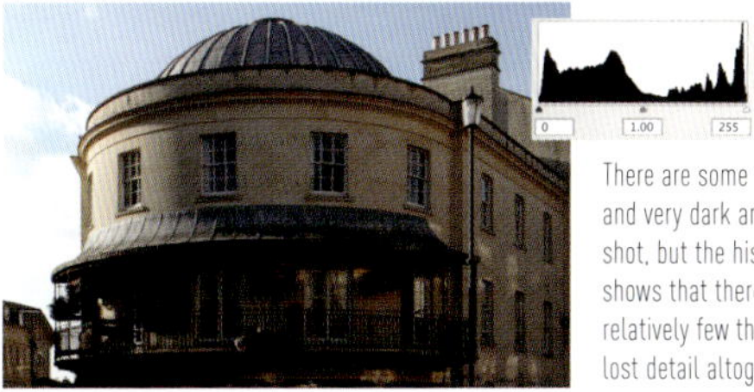

There are some very bright and very dark areas in this shot, but the histogram shows that there are relatively few that have lost detail altogether.

Expose for the highlights

Even today's sophisticated DSLRs can sometimes struggle when attempting to capture a scene containing very bright highlights and dark shadows. When the natural contrast range of the scene exceeds that of the camera, it's simply not possible to record detail in both highlights and shadows.

When this happens you have various options. First, if it's the sky that's causing the problem, fix a neutral graduated filter to the front of the lens to help balance the highlights and shadows (see page 113). Alternatively you could take two or more shots of the same scene, exposing in turn for the highlights and shadows, and combine them in your computer to make a High Dynamic Range (HDR) image (see page 92-93). If neither of those options is possible, then the best option is to expose for the highlights. Take a light reading from the brightest element of the composition (ideally using the spot or partial metering mode), keep the shutter release button semi-depressed to retain the exposure reading, recompose the shot, and fire the shutter. Check the results on the camera's LCD screen, using the histogram, the image replay, and highlight alert functions. Ideally, you'll have recorded detail in the brightest parts of the scene, leaving the darkest areas (hopefully not too many) pure black.

Although filled-in shadow areas are not ideal, they are visually far less distracting than areas of detail-free white. Furthermore, particularly if you have shot using the Raw format, you may find that you can retrieve some detail from the shadows during post-production, whereas blown highlights are rarely recovered.

Of course, there are exceptions to this rule, notably if the highlight areas are small in relation to the shadows or if the detail in the highlights is not necessary to convey the image (such as specular highlights). Generally, when push comes to shove, expose for the highlights.

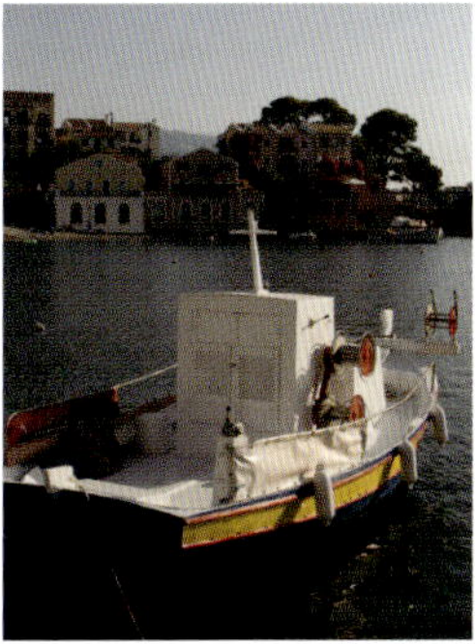

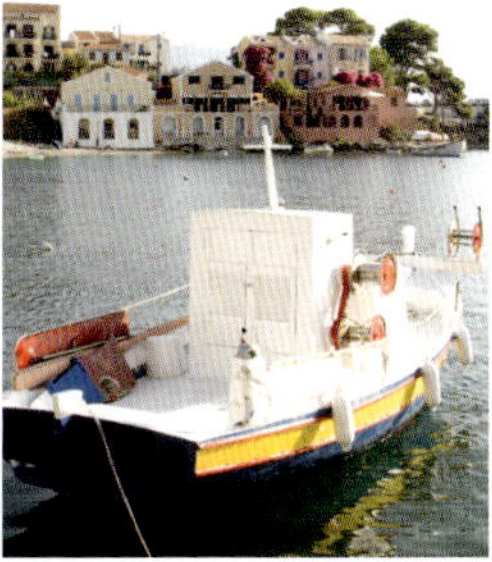

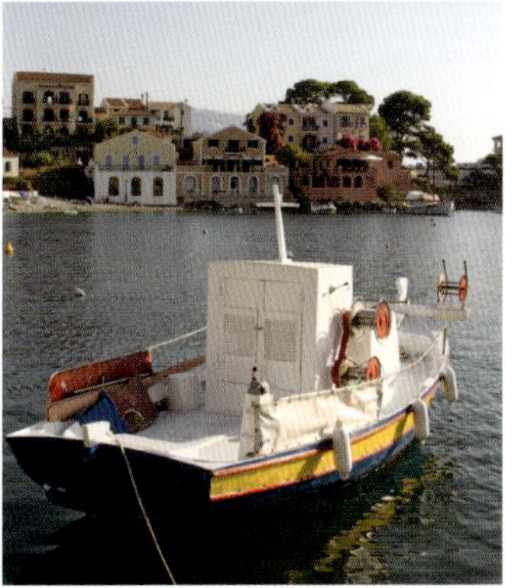

Exposing for both the highlights on the boat and for the sky has left the remainder of this image looking quite dark. However, exposing for the background (above) has resulted in blown highlights in the sky and the boat, which can't be recovered.

Holding the highlights gives you the chance to brighten the shadow regions using your image-editing program.

Expose to the right

Although superficially this may sound similar to the previous tip there is a subtle and important difference. The "right," of course, refers to the right-hand side of the histogram, the highlight area. So why should we want the histogram to show a lot of brightly exposed pixels? Aren't we trying to mke sure highlights aren't blown? Wouldn't it be safer to expose to the left, or underexpose? Well, although it might be safer, if undertaken with care—so the highlights aren't actually blown, or clipped at the right-hand edge of the histogram—exposing to the right, or slightly overexposing, improves the signal-to-noise ratio (SNR) in the shadow regions. The result is less noise in the darker tones—where it is usually most apparent—when the image is later edited on computer.

Exposing to the right works best for images with a lot of shadow or mid-dark tones and, as previously indicated, only if you intend to edit them. Also, again you'll reap greater benefits shooting Raw files, which, as 12-bit or even 14-bit files, contain more color information. Open the Raw file in your Raw conversion program and adjust the brightness levels so that the histogram is spread more evenly across the tones before opening the file in your image-editing program. The image will now look less overexposed, without introducing noise in the shadow regions.

This sequence of shots and accompanying histograms illustrates how, if you're careful to avoid clipping highlights, exposing to the right can result in a better signal-to-noise ratio in shadow areas. The first shot shows a good spread of tones, but with a large shadow area in the foreground. When trying to lighten this area in post-production, noise is introduced and the colors become muddy. In the second shot, the image has been overexposed slightly, while still holding the highlights. When the image is amended in

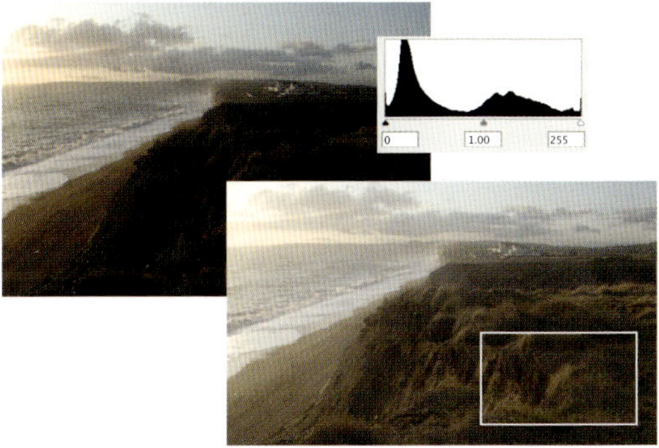

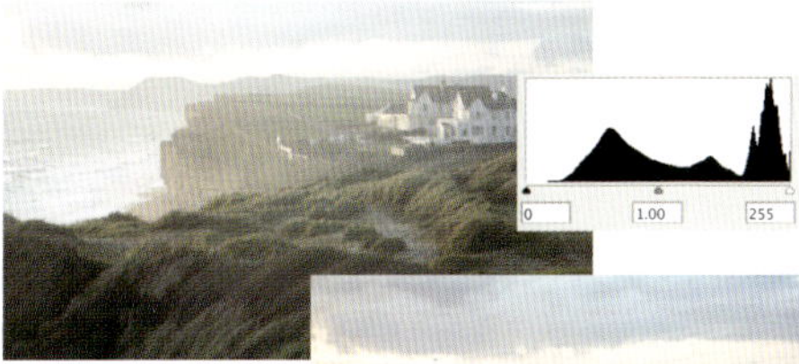

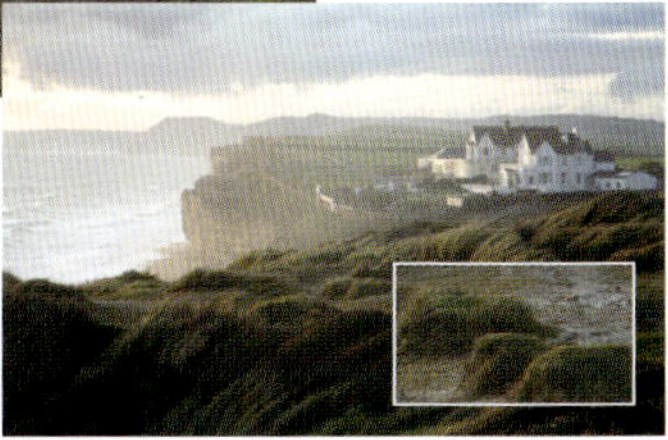

post-production to balance the tones, far less noise is introduced into the foreground shadow region, and the colors are more accurately rendered.

Simplify the scene

There have been lots of books written about unlocking the secrets of good composition, and of course to a certain extent it is a very subjective issue. But there are certain guidelines that you can bear in mind when composing your images, and keeping it simple is one of the best. If, as many of us new to photography are tempted to, you shoot whatever you see

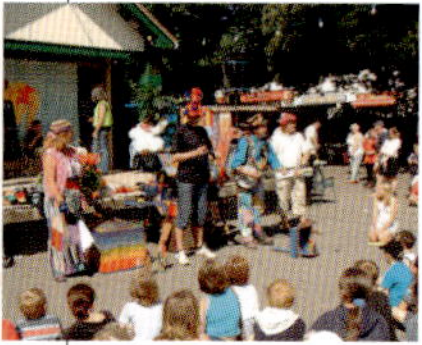

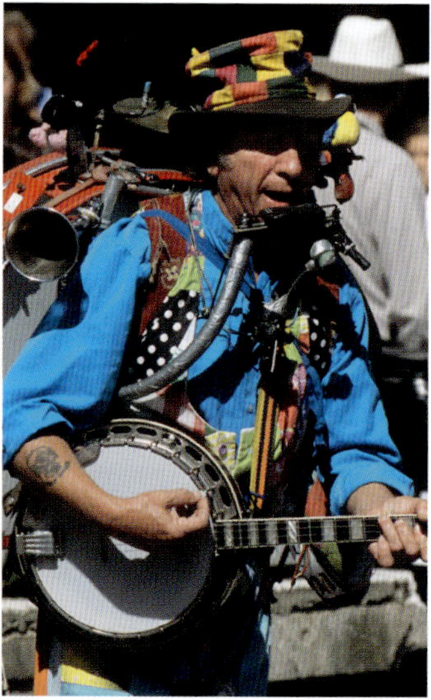

This is a typical scene in which everyone gets their cameras out. The street carnival has pictures at every turn; colorful entertainment and happy spectators abound. But including everything in a single shot doesn't work—the result is too cluttered. Better to find a viewpoint, zoom in, and simplify the scene. Here, the obvious shot is the psychedlic one-man band.

before you, you're likely to end up with a disappointing image that fails because it lacks emphasis. In most cases, your pictures will become stronger if you frame the shot so that there is only one main focal point in the image. Often, you can frame a subject so that it appears alone in the frame; however, if you include further elements, these should complement the main subject, adding to the detail of the story, rather than competing for our attention.

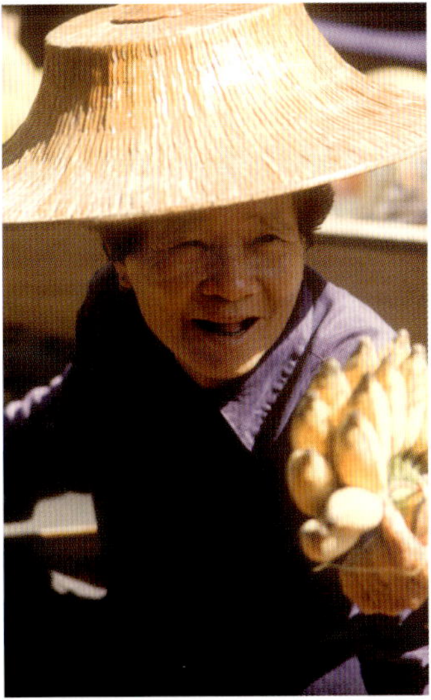

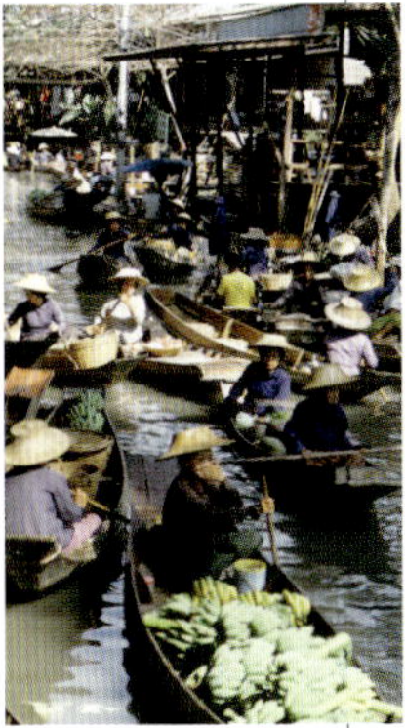

The wide shot of Bankok's floating market gives a good idea of the hustle and bustle of the scene, however it is the shots of individual traders that provide the best results.

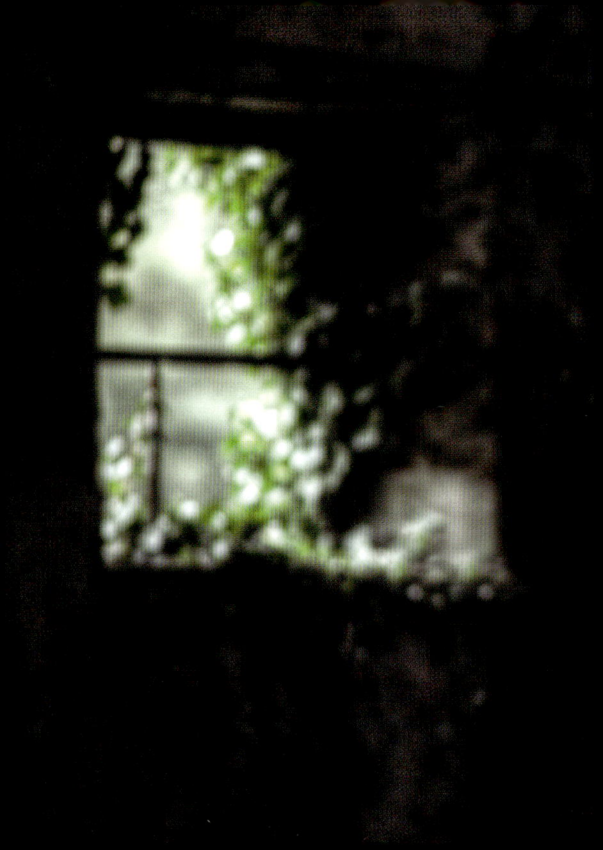

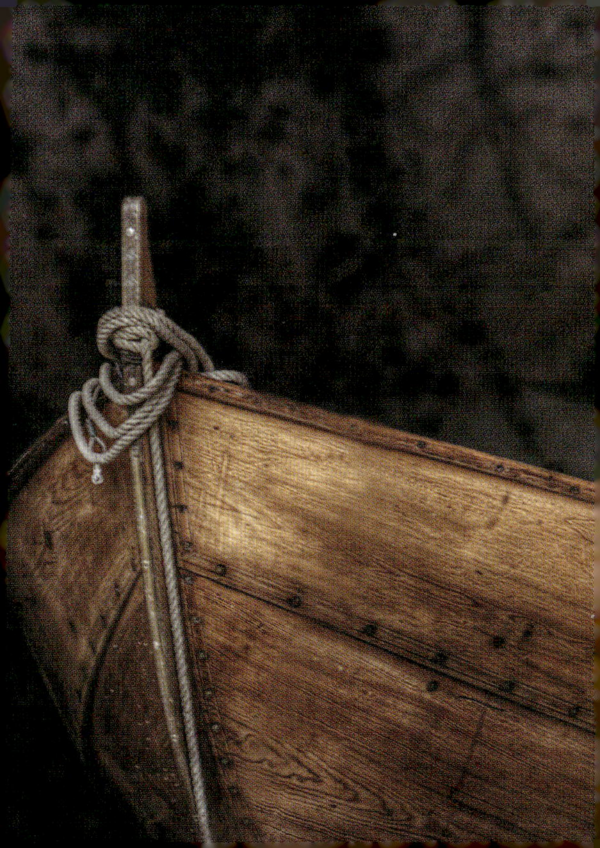

Get in close

Following on from the theme of simplification, another good way to dispense with unwanted and unwarranted clutter in your images is to "get in close." This was the mantra of the famous war photographer Robert Capa, and it's an excellent piece of advice. The advances in modern lens technology, with most zoom lenses now capable of providing good image quality, ensure there's no excuse not to get right up close to your subject; and if you're still not close enough you can always use your legs.

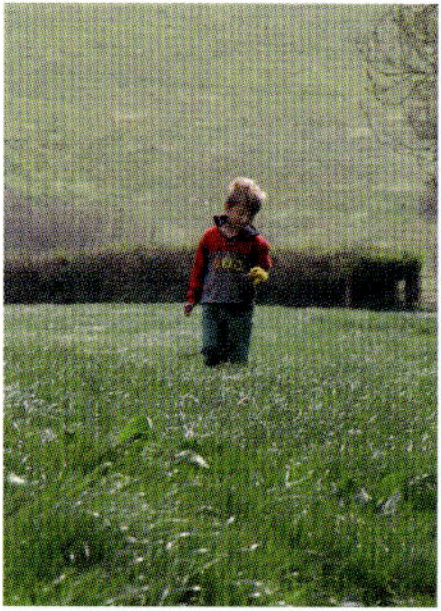

While there's nothing inherently wrong with the top picture of the boy walking through the fields, the close-up image of the girl has greater impact and a less-cluttered composition.

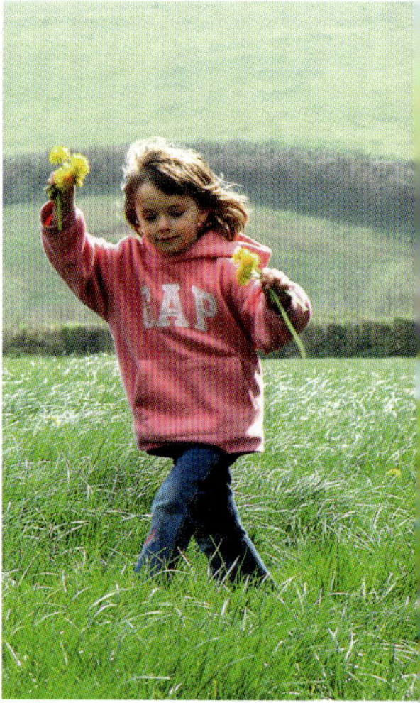

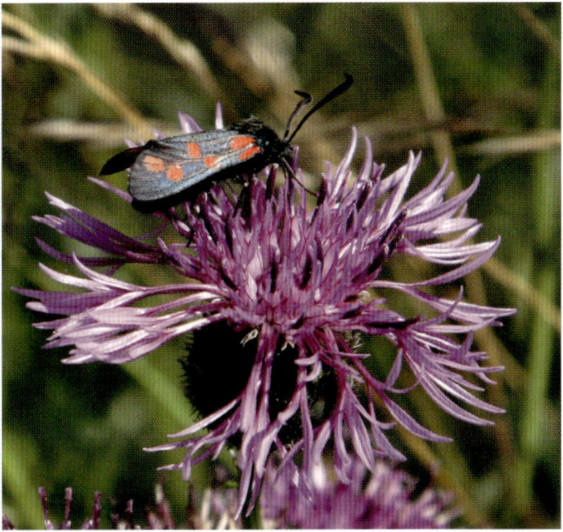

Getting in close with small natural history specimens is essential, otherwise the subject may well get lost among other elements in the composition. Remember also, the closer you get, the narrower the depth of field, which can help further to isolate the subject.

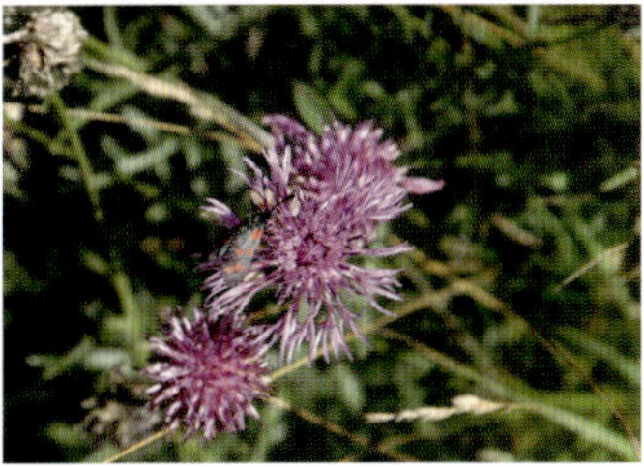

Experiment with format

Digital SLR cameras are designed to be used primarily in the horizontal (or landscape) format. However, they work perfectly well if turned through 90°, and shooting in the vertical (or portrait) format should be something you do quite frequently, even with subject matter that traditionally is shot in either one or the other format. It might feel uncomfortable at first, but it will soon become second nature.

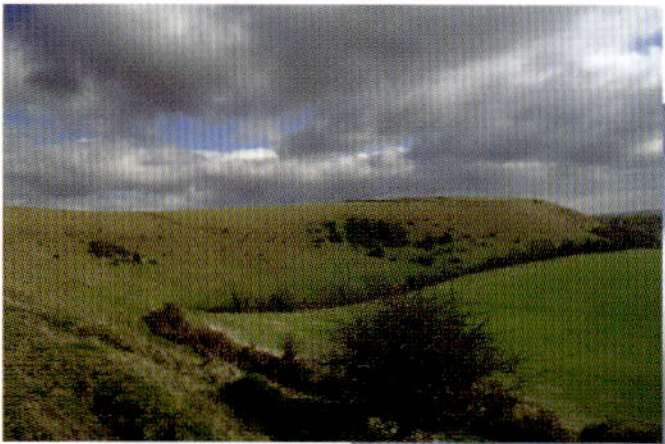

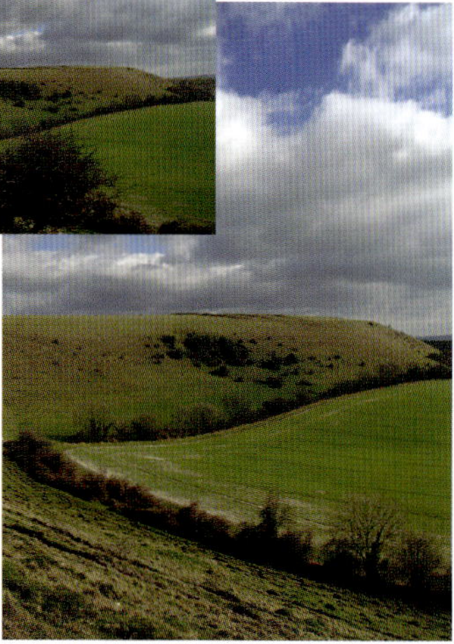

It's all too easy to fall into the trap of thinking that a particular subject will work best with one format, but it is better to try out both if you have the time. Here the composition benefits from not using the more obvious landscape format.

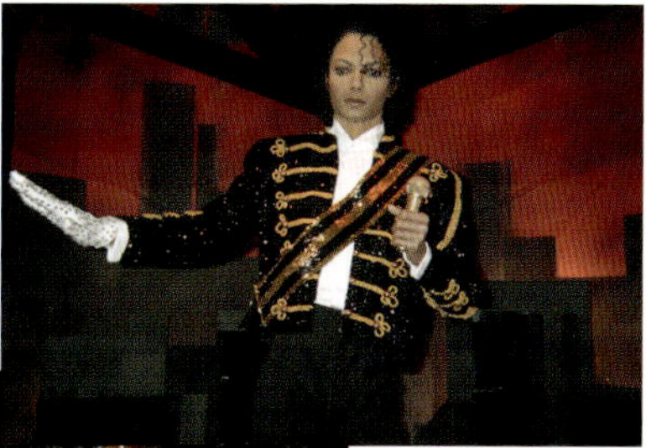

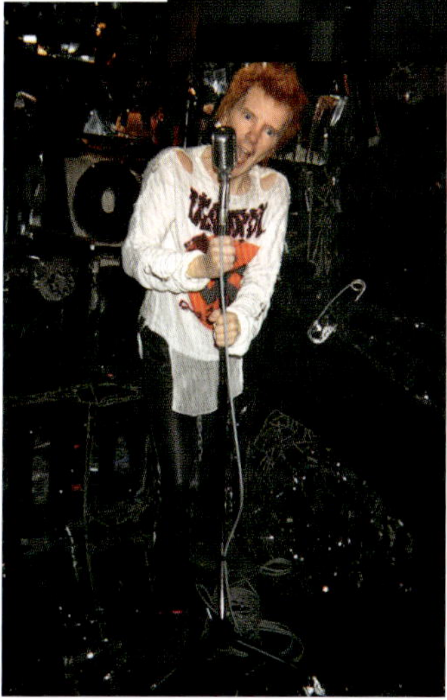

Often the subject dictates which of the two formats you should use. For these shots taken in a waxwork museum, the portrait format was more effective for the shot of former punk rocker Johnny Rotten, while Michael Jackson's pose suggested shooting in landscape format.

Look for form and outline

Shape is perhaps the most significant element in identifying a subject, but it is important to distinguish between three-dimensional shape (form) and two-dimensional shape (outline).

It is helpful to emphasize form in most types of photograph, because otherwise a subject can end up looking like a lifeless card cutout. The shadows in a picture provide the best clues about three-dimensional form: if some surfaces are in the shade, while others are lit, we know that they are at different angles to the light. Rounded surfaces, meanwhile, can be identified by a gradual change in tone.

Outline can be emphasized to depict a subject with graphic simplicity—although by doing so, information about form can be lost. The classic example of a photograph that accentuates shape is the silhouette, but how identifiable the subject is depends on the camera angle—a face, for instance, can be recognized better in profile than when seen from the front.

The shadows on the turrets make it obvious that this is a photograph of a French chateau, and not just a simple drawing in a fairytale story. The subtle gradation of shades between light and dark help to distinguish the round towers from the octagonal one.

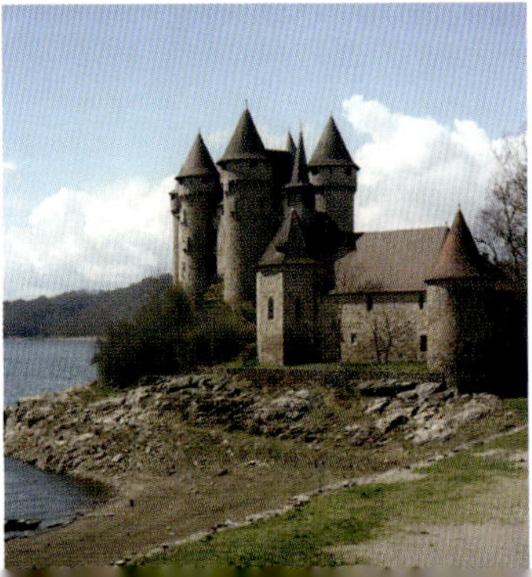

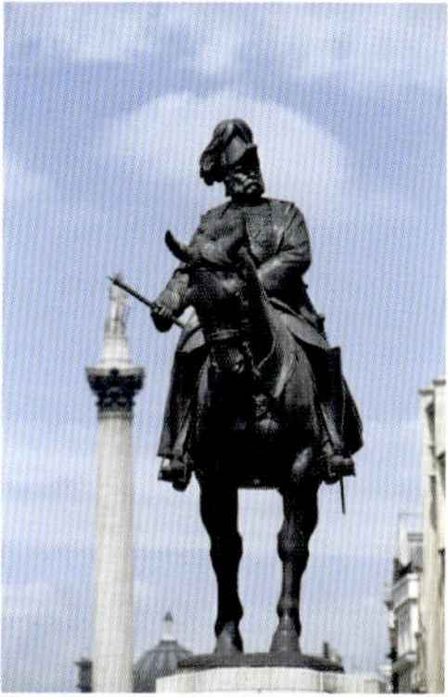

By combining sidelighting with a plain background, outline and form can be shown successfully in the same picture.

The effectiveness of shape as a compositional strategy depend upon camera viewpoint. In these two shots, the rear view of the beast has humor, but is of little use for identification purposes. The profile shot of the Southern White rhinocerous gives a much clearer view.

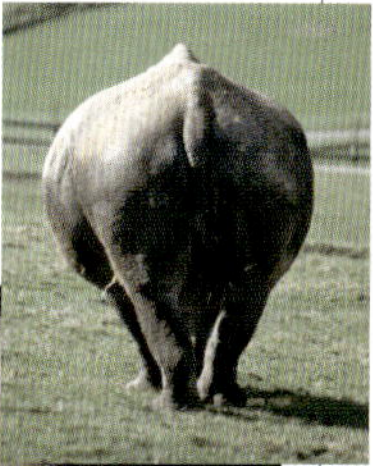

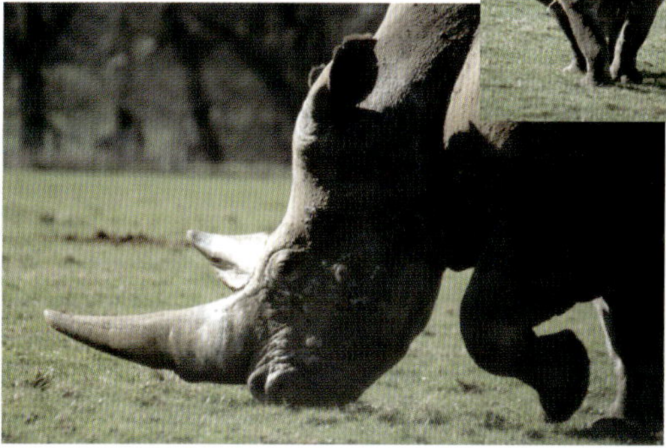

Look for texture

Texture is the picture element that tells you what a subject would be like to the touch; it helps to differentiate the rough from the smooth, to tell feathers from fur. It is the indentations on a surface that give this information, and their presence is shown in a picture by a tell-tale pattern of shading.

Because texture tends to be found on a miniature scale, and relies on good resolution to be seen, it is best accentuated by getting in close to the subject, otherwise the texture can be lost.

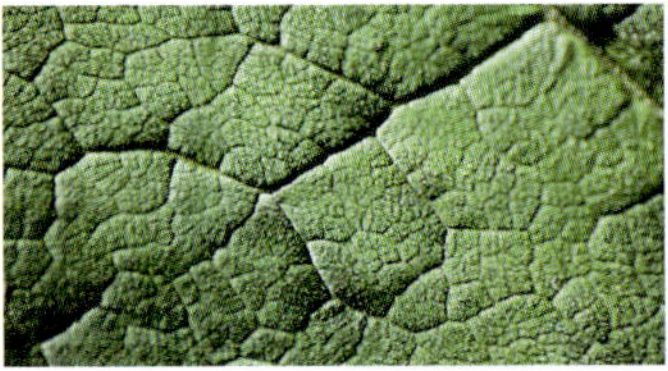

Contrasting light on this section of the leaf gives an accentuated idea of the rough surface of the giant, rhubarb-like pond plant, Gunnera Manicata.

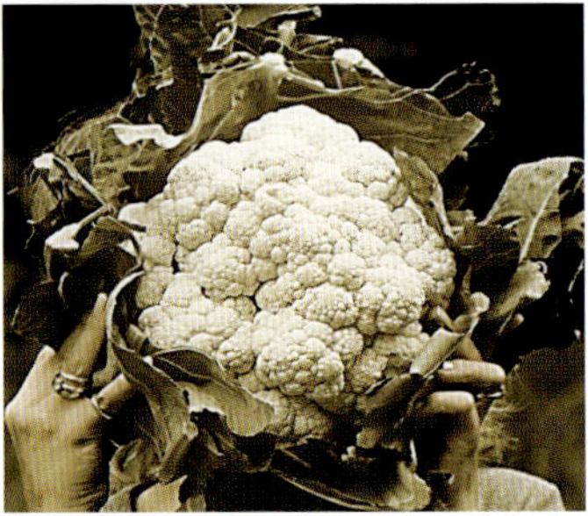

It is possible to accentuate the texture of a subject by image manipulation. The cauliflower florets create a multifaceted surface that looks great in photographs, and to make the most of this, the white part of the vegetable was selected and sharpened using an image-editing program.

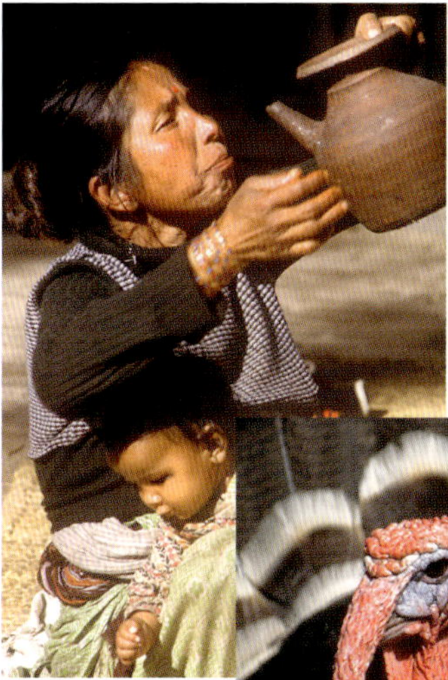

Texture is an important element in portraiture, as it allows us to tell a person's age from the smoothness of their skin, or the presence of wrinkles. In some cases, you may want to emphasize the lines of a face in a portrait, in others the sitter may pay to minimize them.

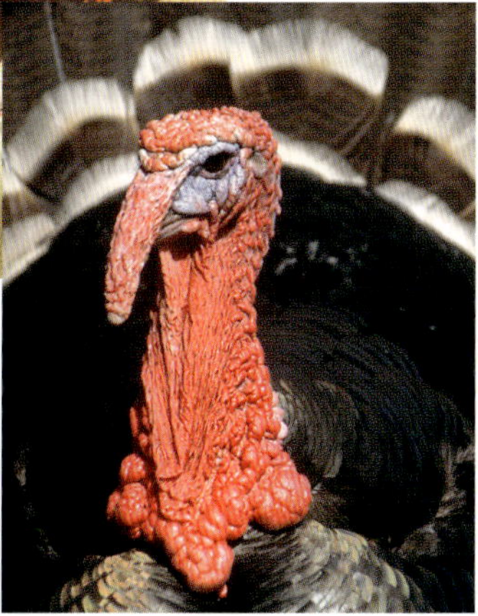

It's not just the red color of this turkey's neck that attracts attention, it is the wrinkly texture too.

Look for pattern

Of all the structural elements within a composition, pattern is perhaps the least obvious to appreciate. The trouble is that pattern is all around us—and not just in wallpaper, tiling, and clothing. Pattern is found in nature, in the bricks of a wall, and on the shelves of a supermarket. Pattern is so pervasive that often we simply don't notice it.

But it is because we're so comfortable with pattern that it makes such a great compostional ally. By placing similar or identical subjects within the same frame, we can create a busy image, but the arrangement is still simple enough to result in a successful image.

Nepalese soldiers waiting patiently for the parade to start. Here is is the break in the regimented pattern that attracts us, with the soldier facing toward the camera becoming the focal point for the picture.

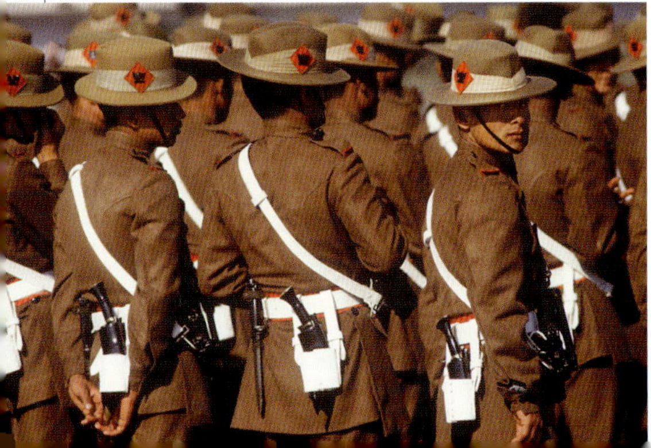

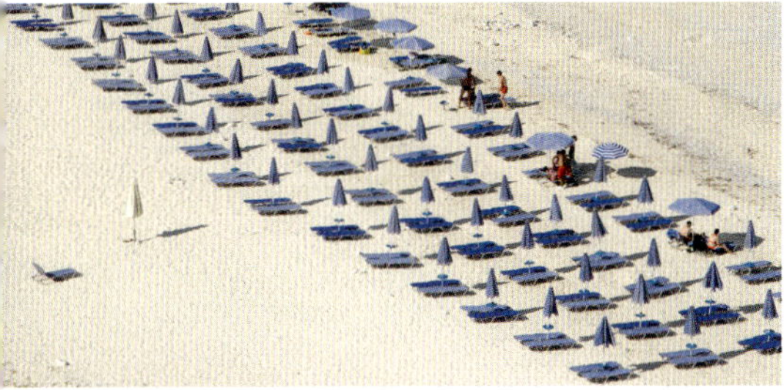

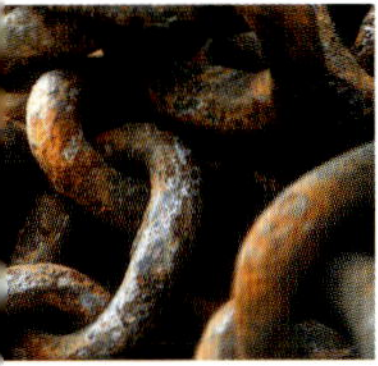

Rusting chains sitting on a fishing wharf. The symbolic nature of the links, and the intense color of the rust, make this a fascinating close-up study.

The uniformly laid out rows of sunbeds and umbrellas on a beach form a graphic image. The uniformity is broken by the single bed and umbrella set out from the rest.

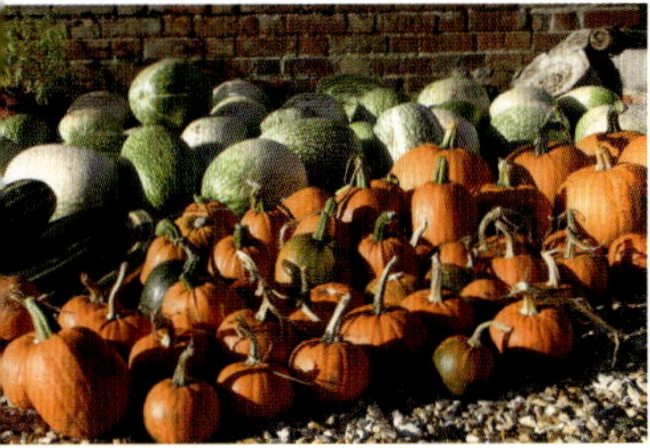

This shot combines the organic patterns of the pumpkins and gourds together with the inorganic patterns formed by the brick wall and the gravel in the foreground.

Look for verticals and horizontals

Lines, whether real or implied, are a fundamental part of composition. They can hold an image together, guiding the viewer's eyes through the image, while at the same time creating dynamic division in the image, breaking it up into discrete sections. Vertical lines, such as trees, tall buildings, and standing figures, bring power and strength to an image, and are often best shot in portrait format, to emphasize their height. Horizontal lines bring a sense of calm to a picture; but avoid placing them in the middle of the frame.

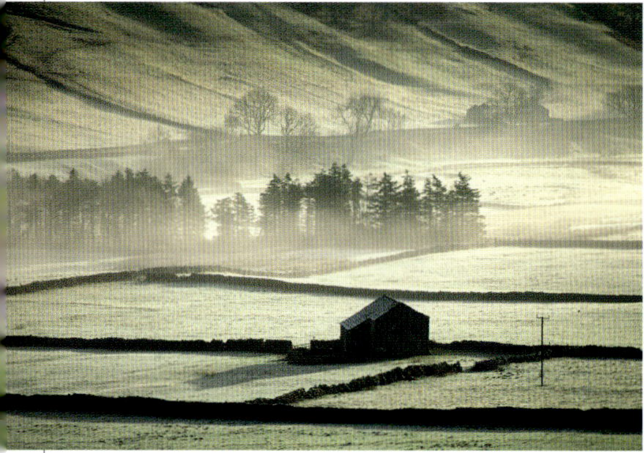

The tranquility of this misty morning shot is reinforced by the horizontal lines formed by the dry stone walls and the line of trees in the middle distance.

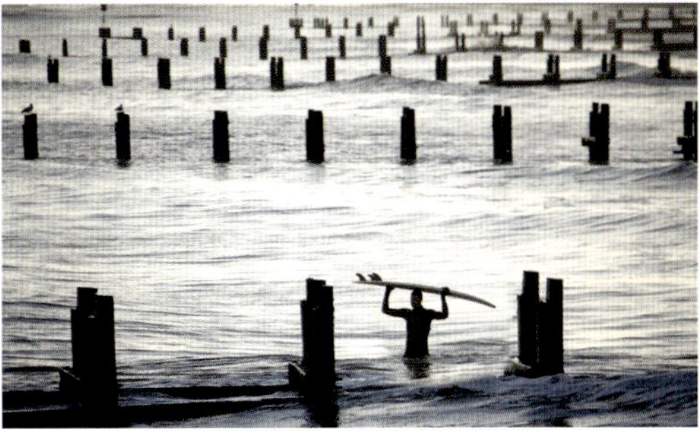

Look for lines, whether vertical or horizontal, in everything you see. The angle of view of this shot results in the partly submerged groynes forming row upon row of horizontal lines, which stretch as far as the eye can see, helping to add depth to this shot.

Strong vertical lines create a sense of the majestic, which is exactly why churches were built with towering lines; they represented the majesty of God.

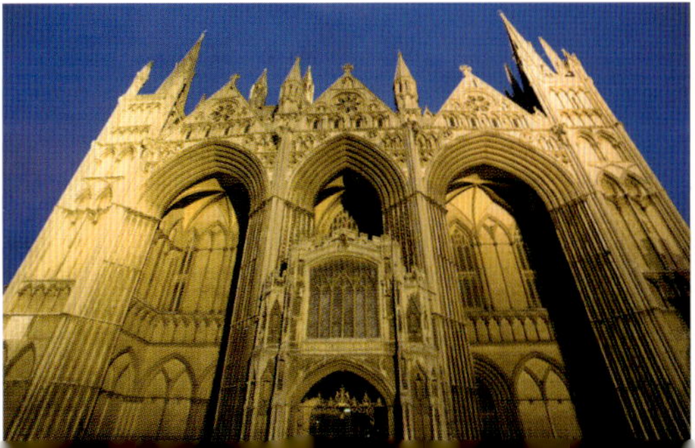

Look for diagonals

Because most photographs are rectangular in shape, diagonal lines play an extremely important part in picture composition. Horizontal and vertical lines, although they can help to "ground" an image, run parallel to the borders and are, therefore, somewhat predictable and static. Diagonals fail to follow the edge of the picture and therefore create visual tension, add dynamism and movement, and lead the viewer through the photo.

This beech forest was full of naturally forming diagonals. A number of the trees were partially blown over, helping to bring different angles to the shot.

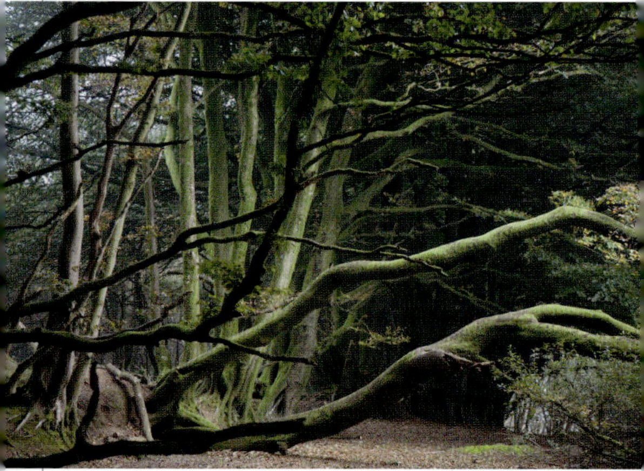

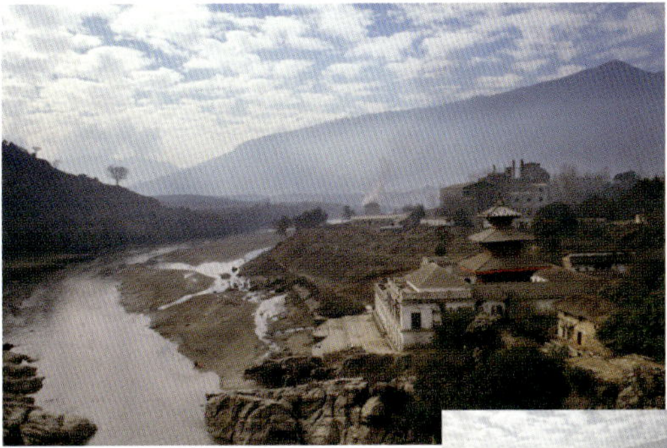

As well as diagonals, curves can lead the viewer into the image in a much gentler way. In landscape photography, curves are particularly useful as you can often engineer the view so that a river or winding road acts as the backbone to the overall composition.

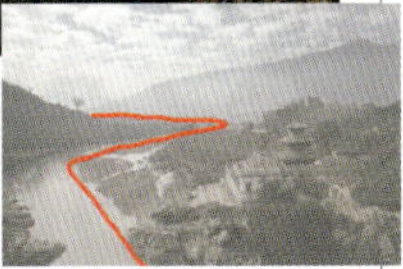

A detail from Berlin's Reichstag. The close camera position helps engineer the strong diagonal line.

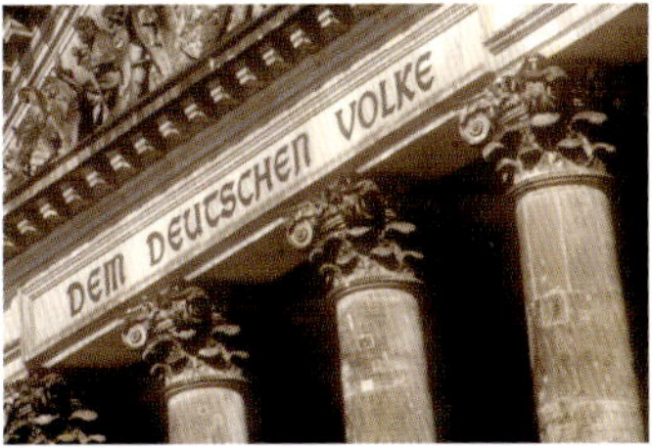

Add depth

A fundamental drawback to photography is that it is two-dimensional. When we look at a photo, we are given no direct information regarding distance and depth. Of course in reality our brains create the missing third dimension, but that information needs to be pieced together from clues in the picture. We can do this quickly and without conscious thought, but the way in which a picture is shot can help to accentuate the three-dimensional experience.

One of the simplest ways of doing this is to make sure the image has an easily recognizable foreground, middle ground, and background. Alternatively use foreground elements as a veil or frame through which to shoot the scene.

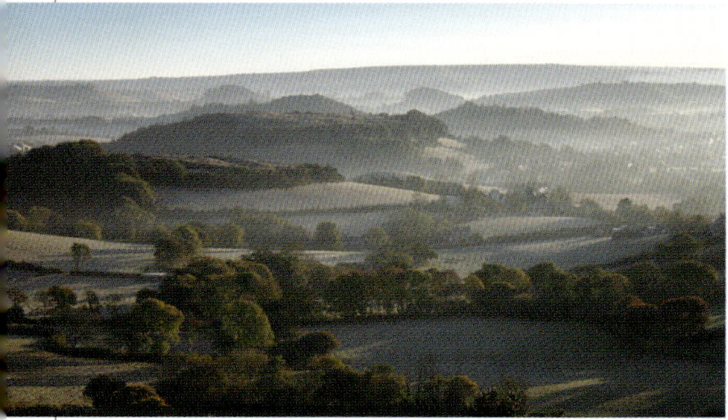

In landscape photography, aerial perspective—in which the more distant an element is from the camera, the less colorful and more hazy it appears—can create a feeling of depth, particularly with a telephoto lens.

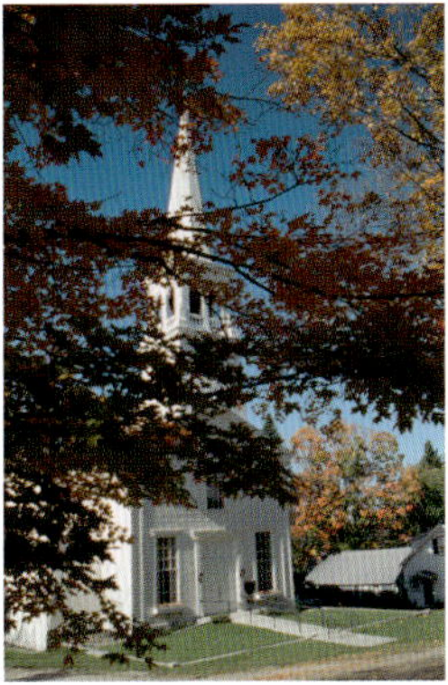

Artists sometimes use a trick known as "overlapping forms" to create a better illusion of depth. The concept is simple; if an element is partly obscured by another, the viewer knows it is further away than the element obscuring it. Here it also gives a less conventional view of this New England church.

The dramatic lighting over this harbor makes the picture, but to avoid an empty foreground a vantage point had to be found so that the rowboat neatly filled the space in the bottom of the frame.

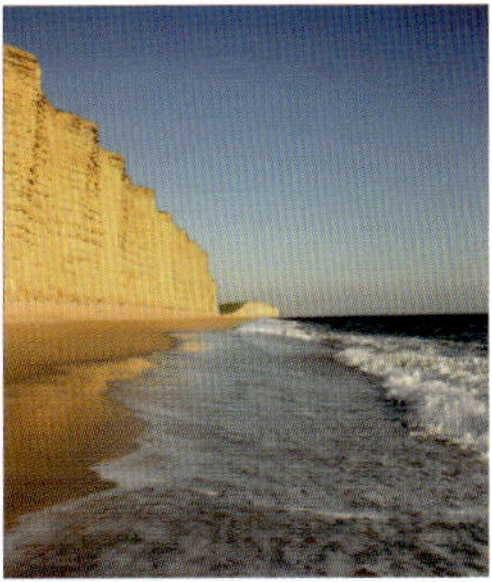

In this shot, the converging lines of the waves and the cliffs to a distant point help create a strong feeling of distance, as well as leading the eye from the foreground to the background.

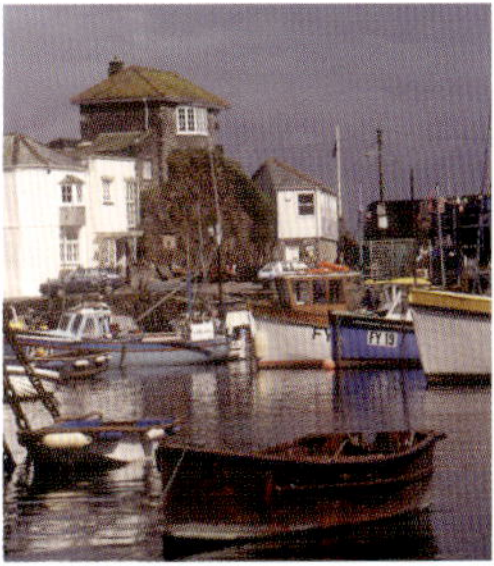

Consider subject placement

Once you have settled on your subject and your vantage point, you next need to consider where to place the elements in the frame. As tempting as it is to place the key focal point in the middle of the frame, you will frequently find that you will get a stronger, more dynamic result if you position the main focus of the image away from the center.

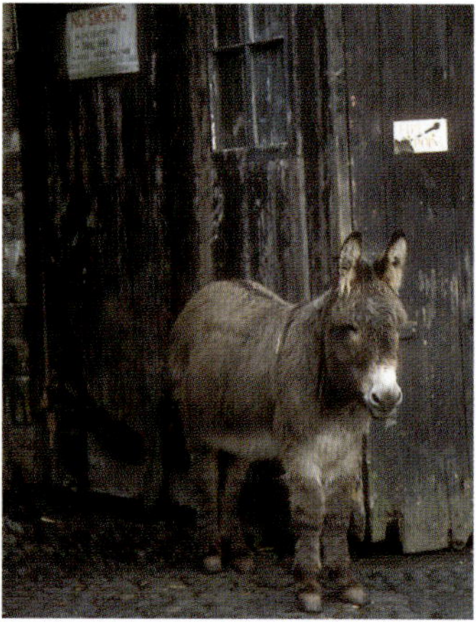

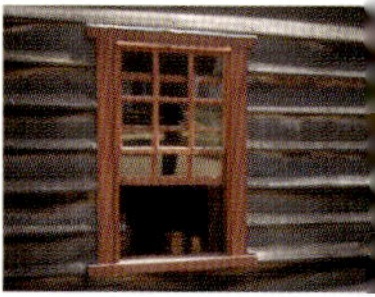

Deliberately placing the main element of a picture off-center creates immediate dynamism even with a simple subject, such as this open farmstead window in Massachusetts.

With animals and people, it is the face—specifically the eyes—that are the focal point of the image. This donkey was placed so that his stable occupied three-quarters of the frame, making his head off-center.

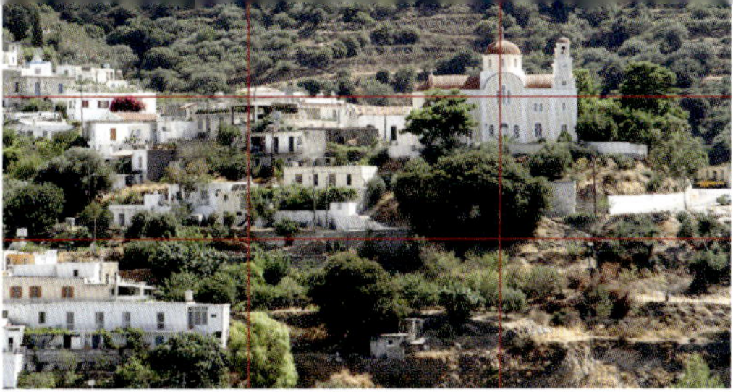

Rule of thirds

The old compositional guideline known as the "rule of thirds" divides the scene into a grid of nine equal rectangles. Place key focal points on any of the four points where these lines intersect, so that they are off-center in both the horizontal and vertical axes.

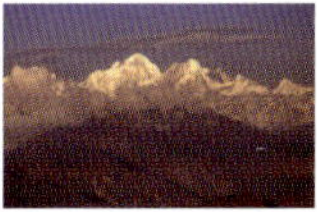

33 PERCENT SKY: The traditional approach places the Himalayan summits along a key rule of thirds line.

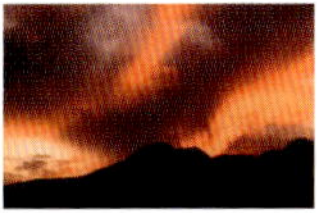

66 PERCENT SKY: A fiery sunset deservedly takes the lion's share of the picture.

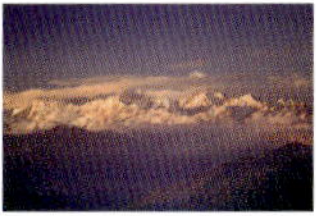

50 PERCENT SKY: A more symmetrical approach can help emphasize tranquility.

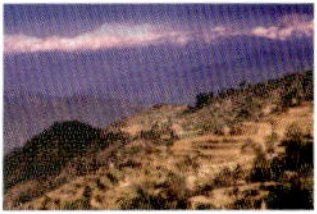

20 PERCENT SKY: This makes amends for the fact that the first ridge splits the foreground and background in two.

Where you place the horizon can have a profound effect on an image. Following the rule of thirds, there are two obvious choices—a third of the way up or a third of the way down. Much will depend on the shot itself, and whether you want to place more significance on the sky or the land.

Vary camera angle

One of the simplest ways of improving your photography is to shoot more pictures. More shots won't guarantee you better images, but can accelerate the learning process. There is little point in shooting the same scene from the same viewpoint, however. You need to work at finding new views of a particular subject. By varying the camera distance and the camera angle, you not only provide different views of the subject, but other compositional elements, such as the lighting, background, and foreground, will also change.

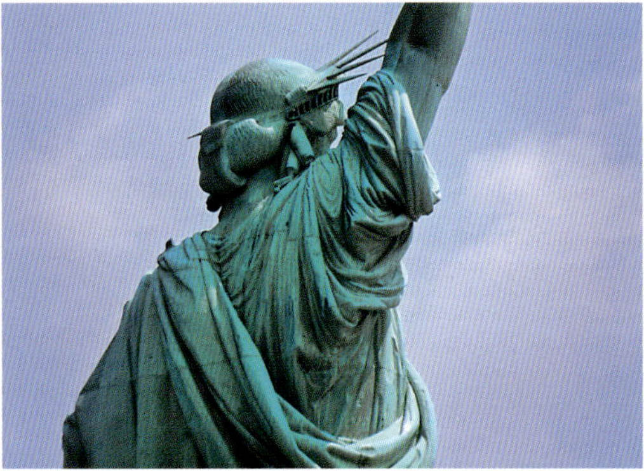

You have the chance to visit some sights and scenes for just a short period of time. Others you can visit at different times of day and in different weather conditions. But even with just a few hours in a single day at a location, you can achieve significantly different shots. The secret is to continually try to find new angles.

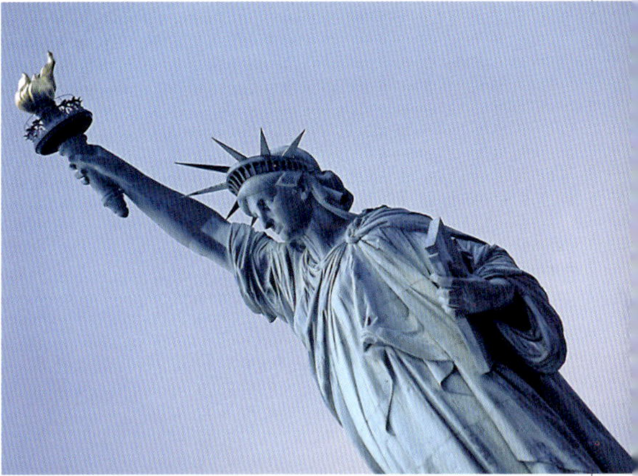

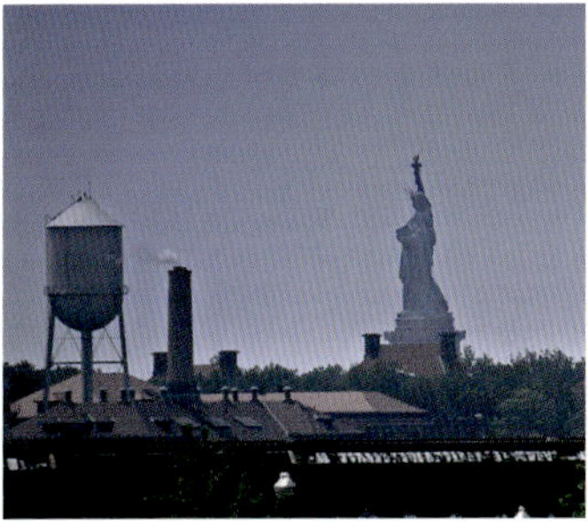

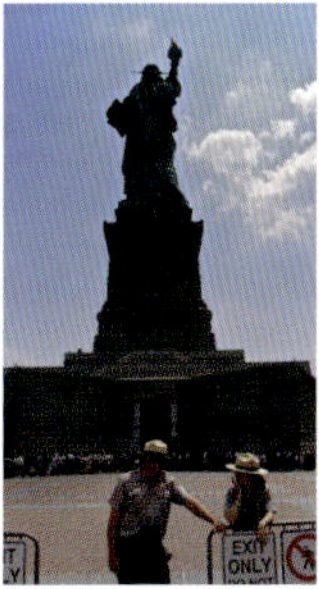
EXIT
ONLY

Vary camera height

It's very tempting to shoot the majority of your pictures from eye level. However, you can add variety to your images by varying how far the camera is from the ground. Good photographers will constantly crouch down or find something to stand on as a way of discovering more interesting shots.

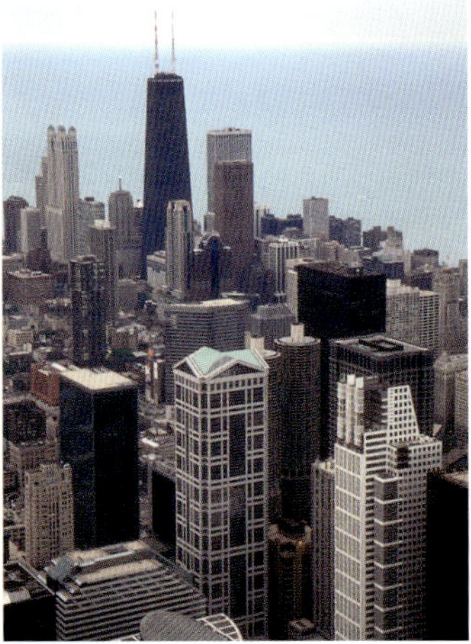

High vantage points allow you to see the spatial relationships between buildings that aren't visible at ground level, as this shot from the Skydeck of the Sears tower in Chicago amply demonstrates.

Seen from above, people, objects, and buildings can look like tiny toy models. This shot was taken from the roof of a French cathedral and deliberately shows the gargoyle's viewpoint.

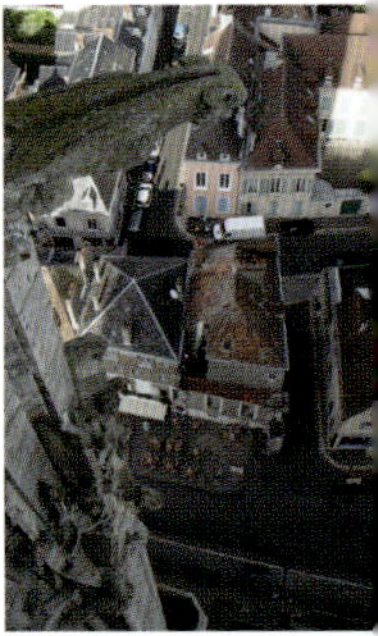

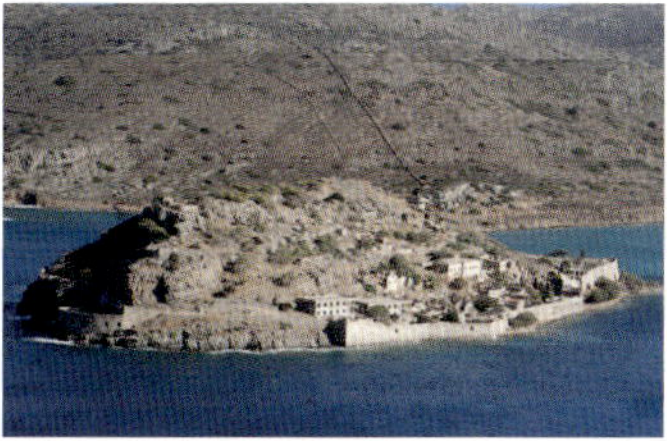

The turquoise sea surrounding the former leper colony on the island of Spinalonga, Crete, is best viewed from the coastal road above.

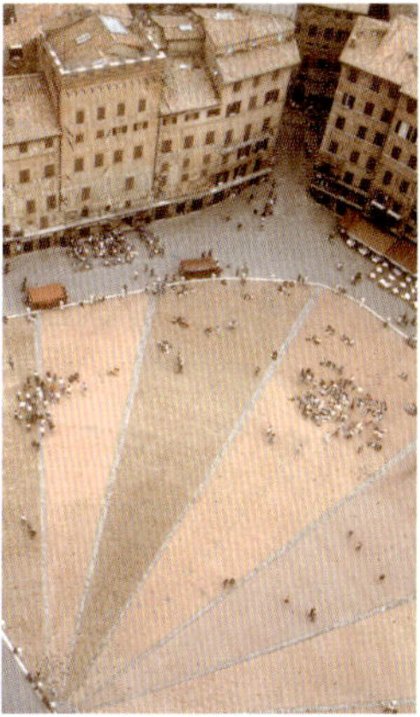

The top of a Tuscan bell tower gives an interesting view of the ancient city below, and is worth the climb.

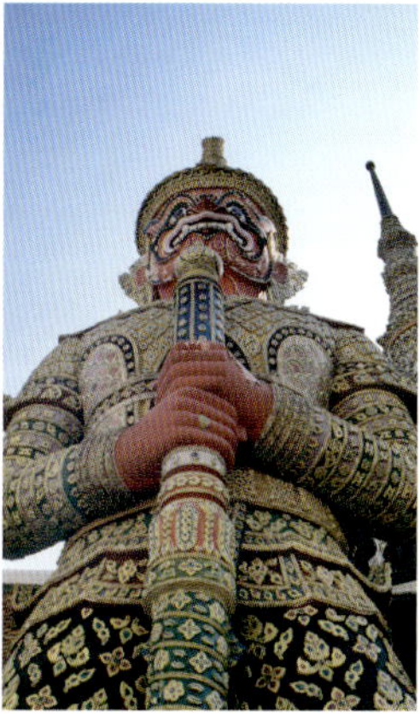

Low-angle views give a feeling of power and size to a subject. This approach brings menace to an ancient Thai warrior statue.

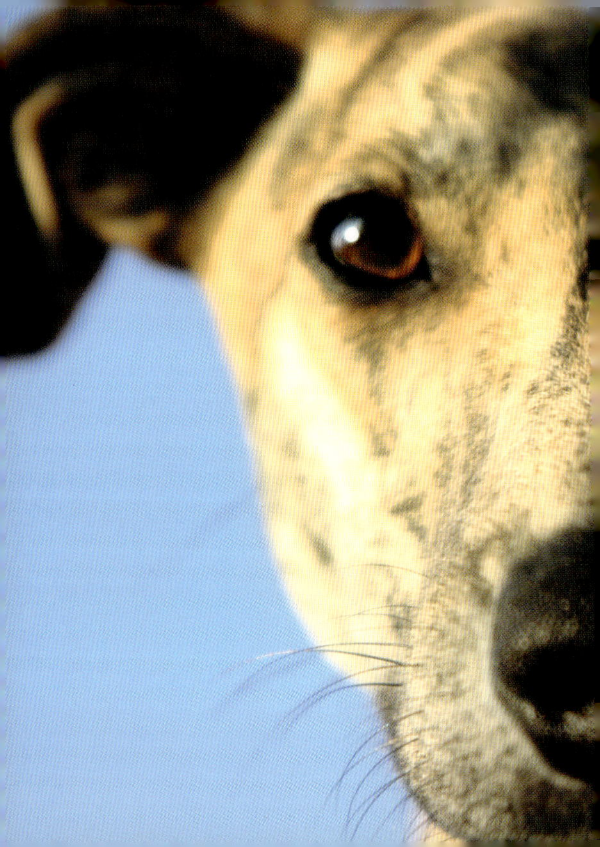

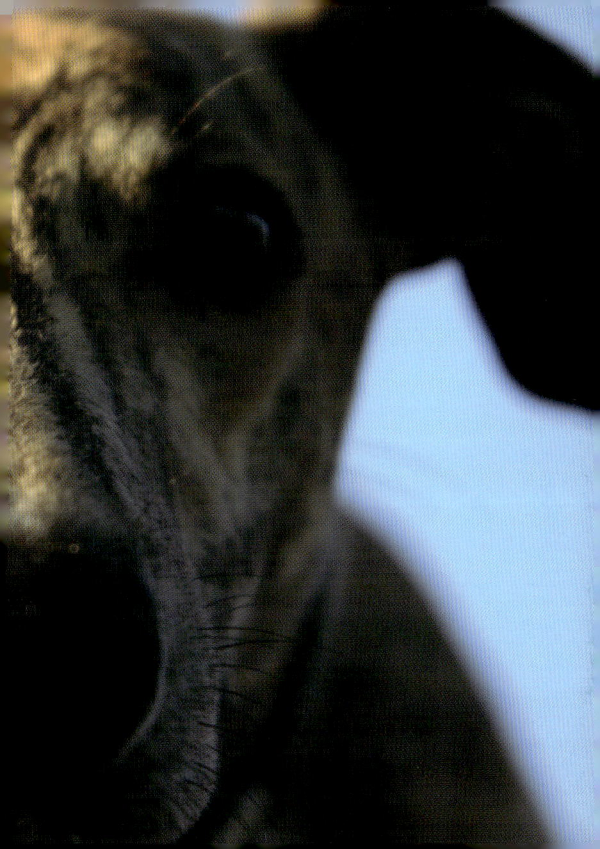

Explore the subject

We've seen how changing camera height and camera angle can provide new and varied perspectives of a particular subject. But it's also important to explore the subject and photograph each element, as these images may reveal an essence of the subject that visually may capture it better than a long shot of the entire subject or scene. Find the detail in a subject that might otherwise be overlooked. This will not only add variety to the series of images, but it may also help to simplify them, often making for a stronger composition.

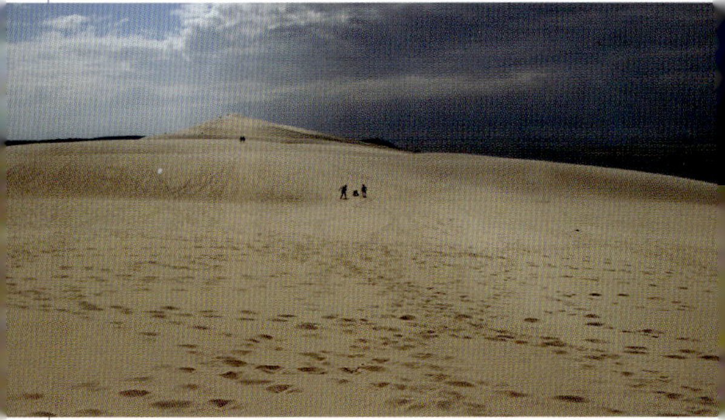

The series of photographs found on these pages show the Dune de Pyla, near Arcachon in northern France. Nearly 2 miles (3 km) long, 1,500 feet (500m) wide, and over 300 feet (100m) tall, it is the tallest sanddune in Europe. The shot above provides a good idea of the size of the dune, but the photographs on the opposite page capture details and other views that help reinforce a sense of place.

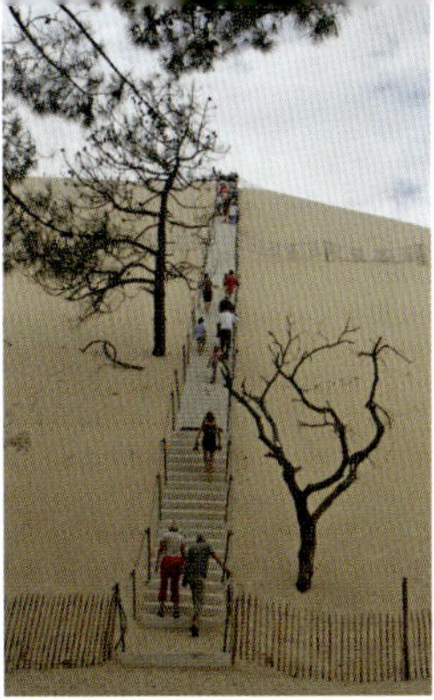

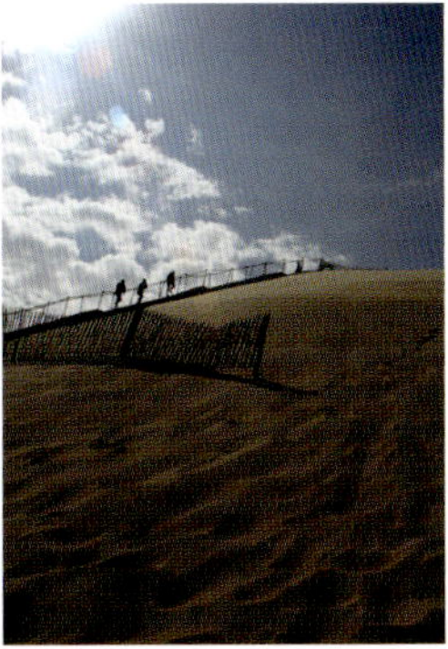

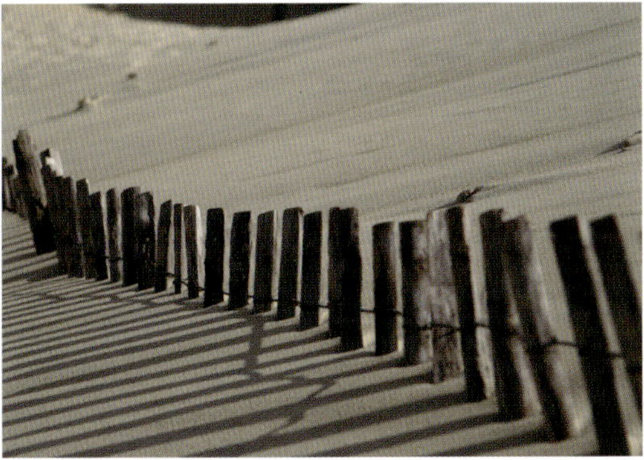

Shoot for post-production

Of course we should always strive to get the best possible shot in camera at all times. But often there'll be occasions when, due to situations outside our control, we should remember what is achievable on computer during post-production. Removing unwanted and unsightly elements and blemishes, or combining two or more images to create a stronger final image is now quick and easy using almost any image-editing software. So, even if things seem to be conspiring against you in pursuit of the perfect shot, think how you can work round this on your computer and what shots you'll need to get the final result you want.

A common scenario: exposing for the land results in an overexposed sky (top right), while exposing for the sky, results in underexposed foreground (bottom right). Taking two shots and combining them on your computer gets the desired final result (below).

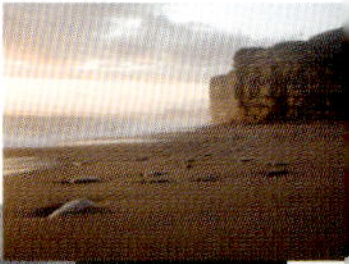

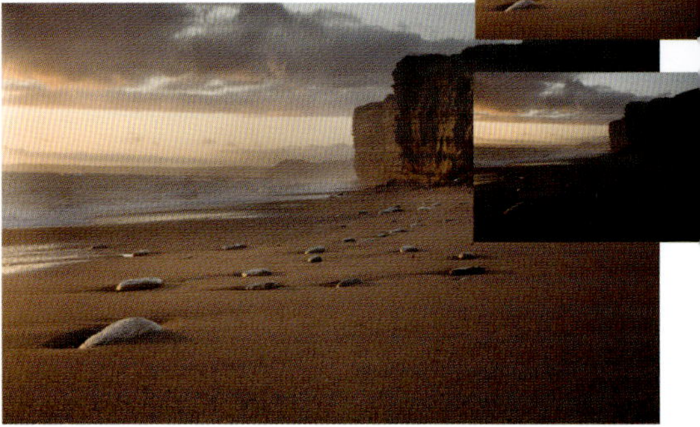

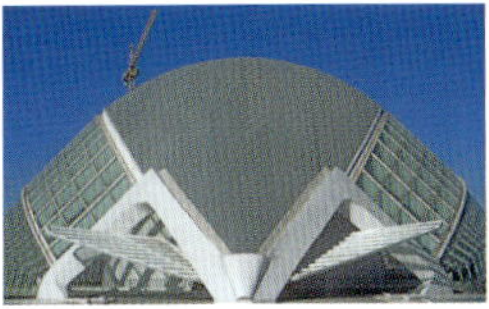

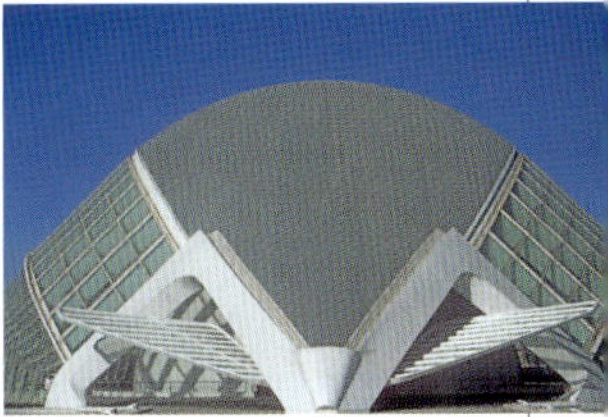

For this shot it was impossible to get a perfectly symmetrical view of the structure without including the crane. Rather than compromising on the viewpoint, it was shot knowing that the crane could be removed in seconds on the computer.

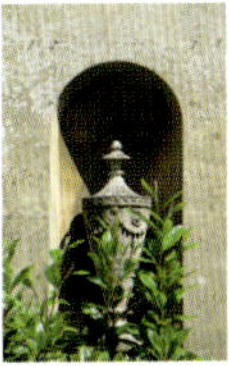

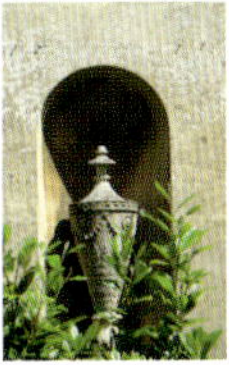

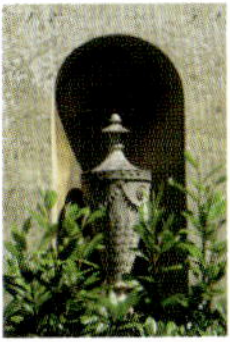

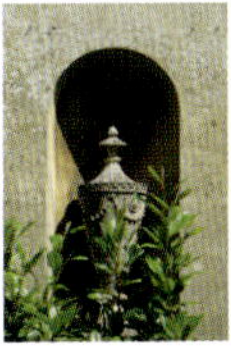

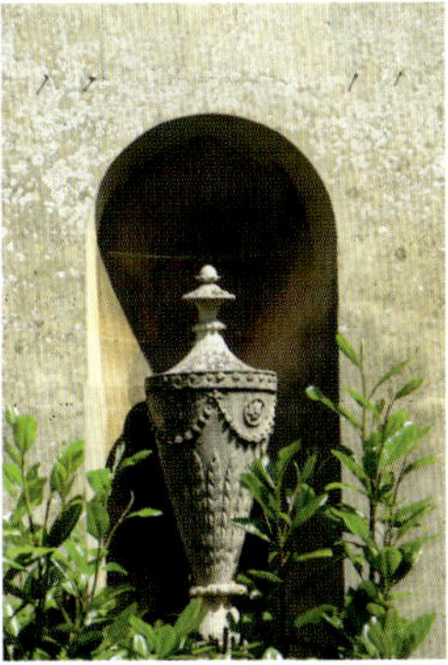

Whatever the camera position, a clear view of the carved urn, free of magnolia branches, could not be found. By taking four shots, a composite giving a much clearer view of the architectural detail could be constructed.

Shoot for HDR

The concept of HDR (High Dynamic Range) imagery, in which a series of progressively exposed shots of the same scene are combined to make one image with the complete tonal range from bright highlights to dark shadows, has been around for many years. Now, with the advent of affordable digital cameras and image-editing programs the process is more popular than ever. And to help, there is software that will combine the images for you and present a single HDR image. The software uses a process known as tone mapping, which enables the monitor to display an approximate representation of the high-dynamic image, which otherwise would be outside the monitor's own dynamic range capability. Results can vary from the highly stylized to the naturalistic.

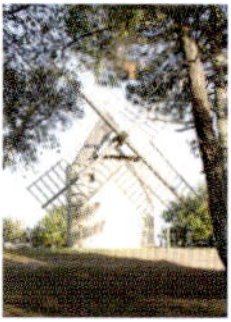
EXPOSURE +2

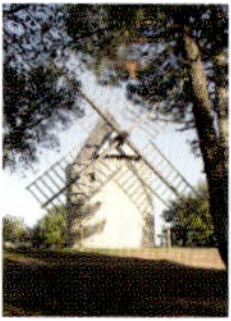
EXPOSURE +1

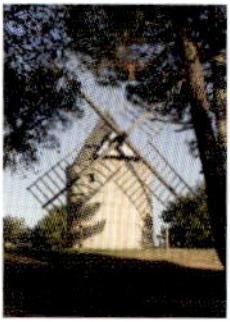
EXPOSURE 0

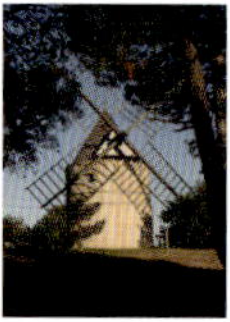
EXPOSURE −1

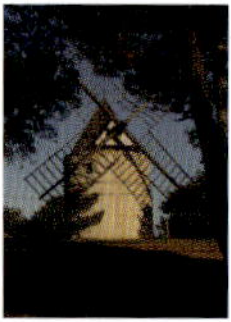
EXPOSURE −2

This series of images shows the same scene. It was photographed five times with the camera on a tripod. The initial meter reading (Exposure 0), revealed some blown highlights on the windmill, so four additional shots were taken, each one either a stop more or less than the previous shot. The result is five separate exposures ranging from +2 to −2 stops. Most cameras will allow you to bracket shots automatically.

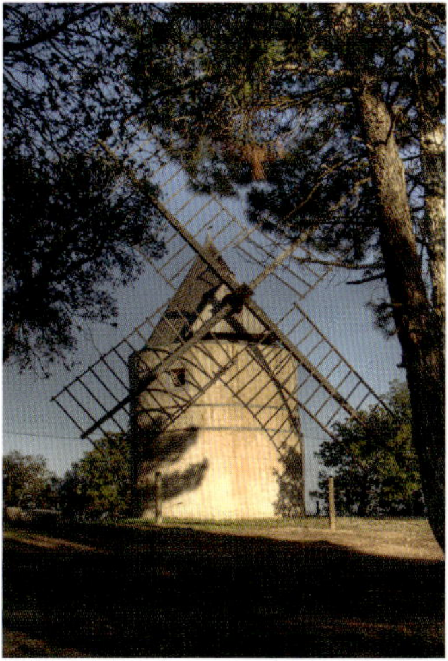

The resulting HDR image as converted by Photomatix (one of the most popular examples of HDR software) shows good shadow detail in the trees and the foreground, while holding the highlights on the windmill. Naturally, because a number of shots are required of the same scene, the process doesn't work when moving objects are present in the scene. However, shooting Raw will allow you to produce "fake" HDR images as you can adjust the exposure in Raw converter software, and create and save five separate exposures from the same shot, or the software will do it automatically for you.

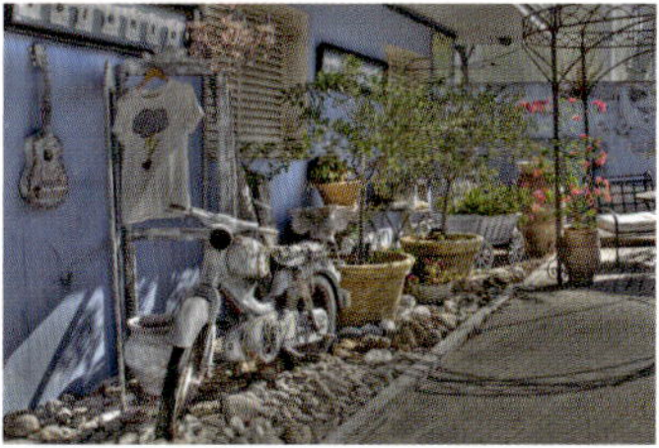

This scene underwent the same process, but by selecting different settings in Photomatix a much more stylized image is the result.

Photographing people

Styles of portraiture vary, but most photographers endeavor to capture a likeness of the human face that does not distort or exaggerate the form of the features. Lighting and lens choice, therefore, are the key. Photograph a person face-on from closer than a couple of meters away, and the perspective will tend to make noses, chins, checkbones, and eye sockets look more pronounced. For close-ups, therefore, it is usual to use a medium-length telephoto lens setting—100mm is ideal.

To complement this approach, the ideal lighting should be reasonably soft: harsh lighting creates unflattering shadows under the nose and around the eyes.

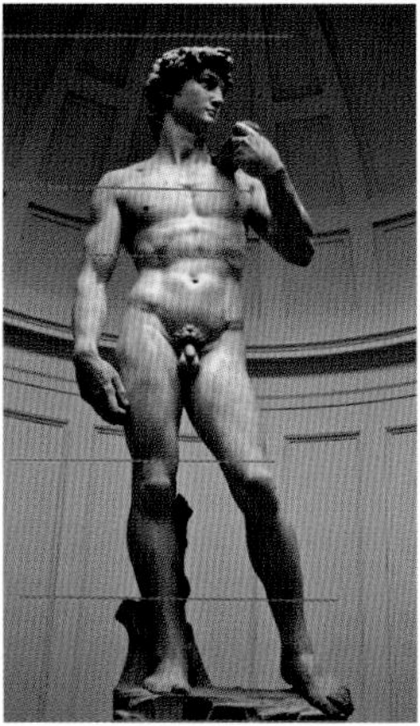

Cutting up bodies

When shooting a close-up of a person's face, you should avoid framing it so that the bottom of the frame cuts through the neck, otherwise your subject may look to have been decapitated. Instead, the base of the picture should be positioned to cut through the shoulders, with a slight gap between the top of the head and the top of the frame.

For wider, fuller figure shots, you should similarly avoid cropping so that the base of the frame cuts through other joints. The image of the statue of David shows where the bottom of the frame should run for a variety of body shots.

When photographing people in profile, you should try to frame the head so it has more room in front of it than behind it. This helps to provide an off-center composition; when we look at a picture of a person photographed side-on, we automatically look across in the same direction that the person in the picture is looking. If the frame is too close to the face, there is not enough "looking space," and the picture will appear cramped.

With more space in front of the man's head than behind it, the image appears much better balanced.

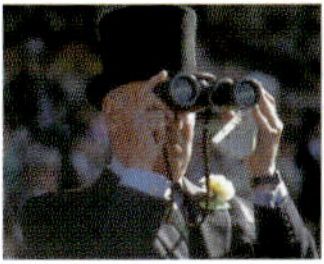

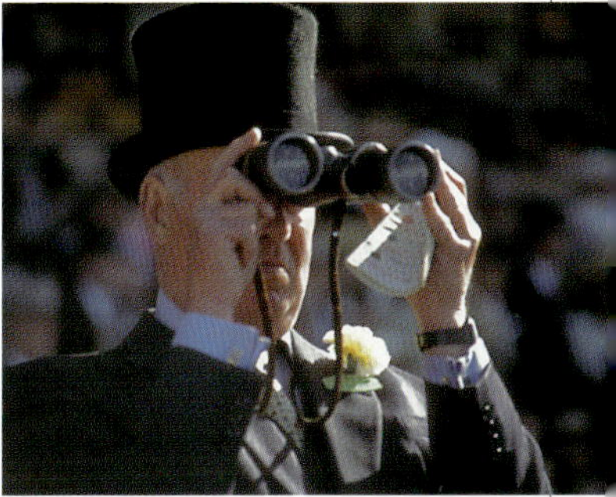

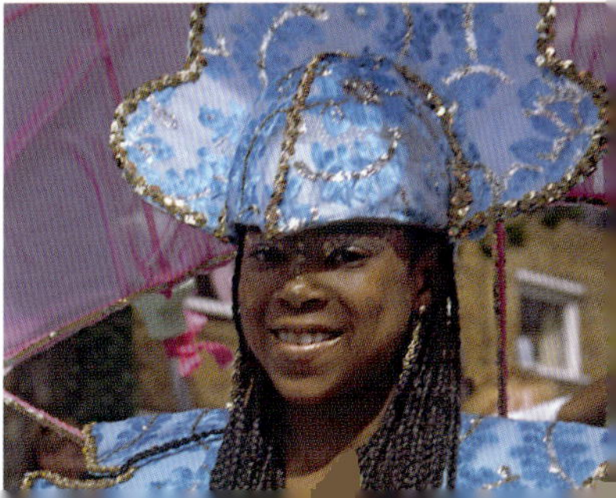

A wide aperture is useful with portraits, to prevent the background from becoming a distraction.

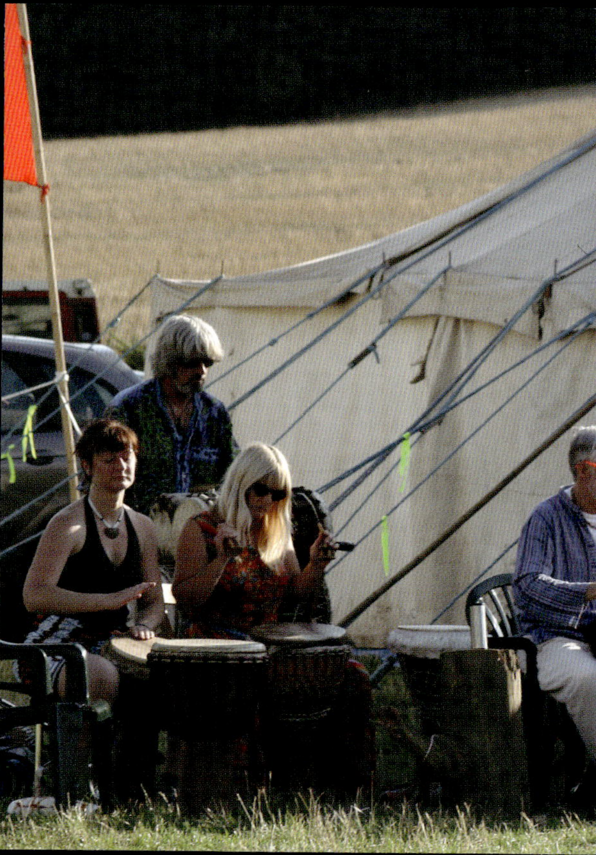

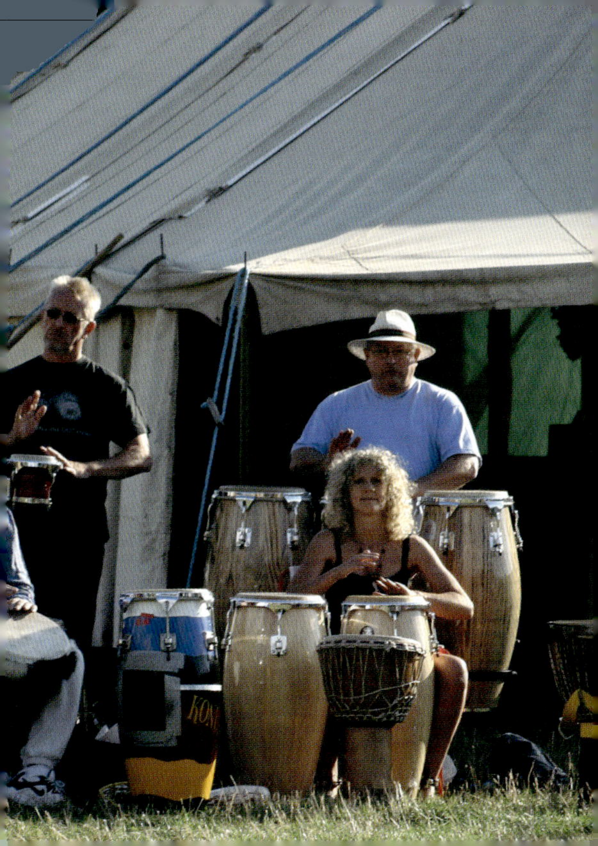

Photographing wildlife

The basic techniques for capturing good wildlife shots can be learned in the garden. Catching sharp, full-frame shots of garden birds, for example, will develop your reactions and focusing skills; images of bugs and butterflies will hone your macro techniques; while shots of a cat or dog can help you develop a sense of the importance of background and expression.

Long focal lengths are essential for successful wildlife photography. For decent close-up shots of birds, an efl of 600mm is normal. With larger animals, you can get away with slightly shorter focal lengths, depending on their size; an efl of 400mm is useful for some larger animals, as it's unwise to get too close to a hippopotamus or lion, whether in an animal park or in the wilds of Africa.

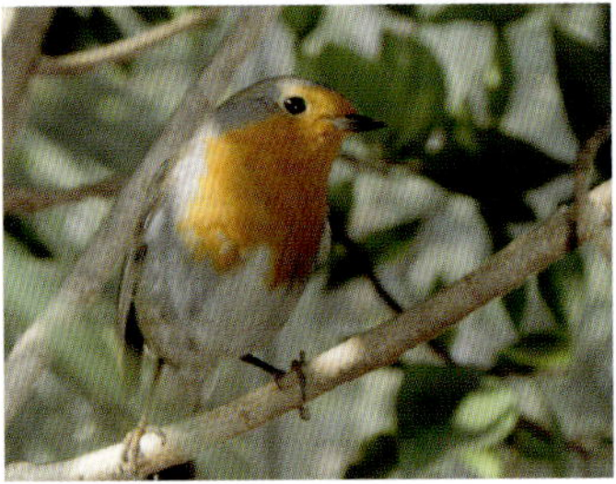

Garden birds present a good subject with which to learn the essential skills of wildlife photography. A robin will perch and pose around the garden, but you have to act quickly in order to get a good picture, and choose a suitable backdrop.

For this Giant Owl butterfly, most standard lens will probably get you in close enough for a full-frame shot. However for decent-sized shots of smaller creatures, a macro lens is an essential piece of kit.

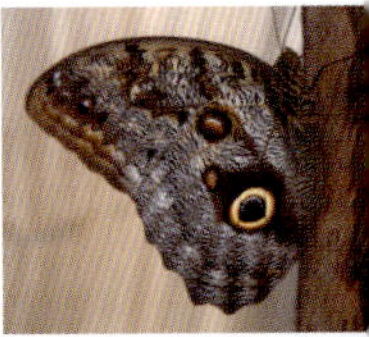

Wildlife kit bag

The ideal camera equipment for the wildlife photographer would include:

- A long telephoto zoom with a maximum efl of 300–400mm for general animal photography.
- A long telephoto prime lens or teleconverter, to provide an efl of around 600mm for bird photography
- A macro lens with 1:1 magnification for close-ups of insects and other small creatures.

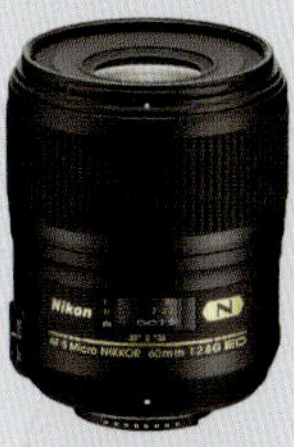

Shooting through bars

Wire fencing, clear acrylic screens, and glass viewing panels can all cause difficulties when taking pictures. It is essential to get these obstacles as out of focus as possible in the shot. Use a large aperture and get the lens as close to the screen or fencing as possible, with the front of the lens actually making contact with the panel if possible. With mesh fencing, make sure that the lens lines up with a hole in the wiring, so the middle of the picture (at the very least) will have an unobstructed view. If may also be necessary to switch to manual focus.

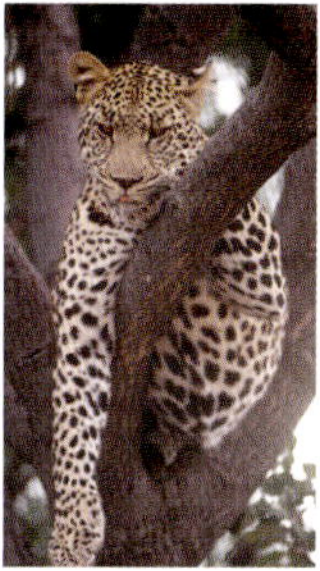

Leopards typically sleep and eat in trees, making this the obvious place to find and photograph them in the wild. Knowing a little of the animal's behavior will help you get better shots.

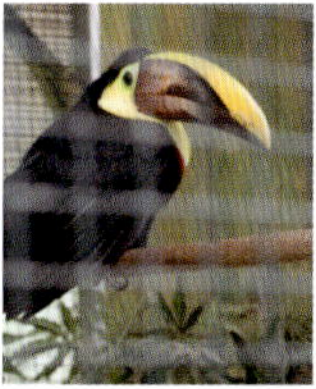

BEFORE

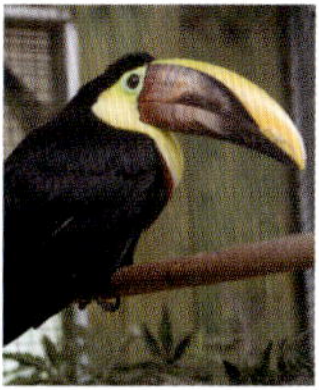

AFTER

Photographing architecture

Although you can use just about any lens for photographing buildings—even telephotos can work if you're isolating detail or sufficently far away to fit the whole building into the frame—the most popular architectural lenses are wide-angle. As discussed on pages 42–43, such lenses are capable of getting more of the subject into the frame, and so are ideal for architecture, particularly when shooting indoors, where the number of possible viewpoints is even more restricted. Fortunately, the one drawback to using wide-angle lenses for architecture—the issue of converging verticals—is easily remedied using image-editing software.

Straightening up

Different image-editing software works in different ways to fix converging verticals. Indeed there is likely to be a number of ways to fix them in the same program. Here, the Crop tool has been used in Photoshop. With the initial crop made, the Perspective box is checked in the Tool Options bar, and the top corner handles dragged in so the the side crop selection lines run parallel to the sides of the building. Click the tick icon to to execute the crop.

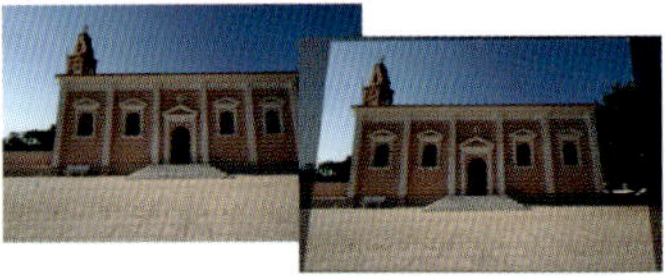

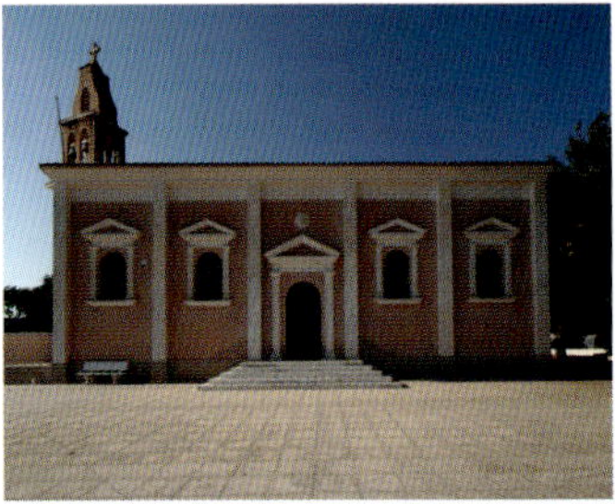

Natural light half way between sidelighting and frontal lighting is ideal for architecture.

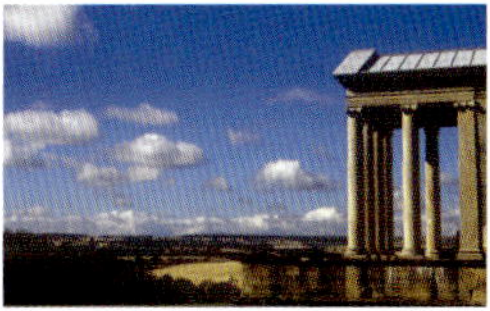

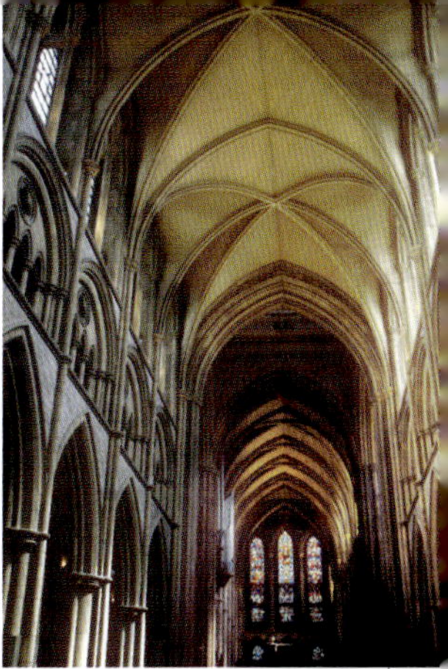

Super wide-angles come into their own with interior photography.

A wide-angle lens lets you show a building in its surroundings. The grasses in the foreground of this ruined castle contribute to the mood of the picture.

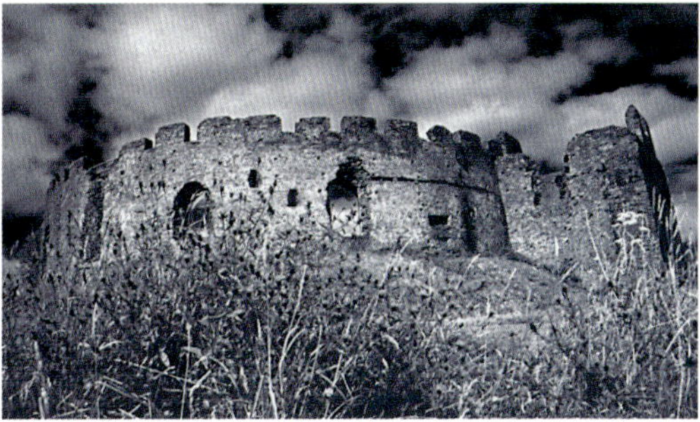

Photographing sports

Vantage point is all-important in sports photography: you have to find a spot that is likely to provide a good view if, and when, something happens. Getting such vantage points can be almost impossible with large sporting occasions, for this reason it's often best to concentrate on lower-league events or minority sports.

Focal length depends largely on the sport. For good close-up shots of field sports, efl 300mm or greater is usually needed. Experiment with shots; try some that freeze the action and others that use creative blur to portray a sense of speed.

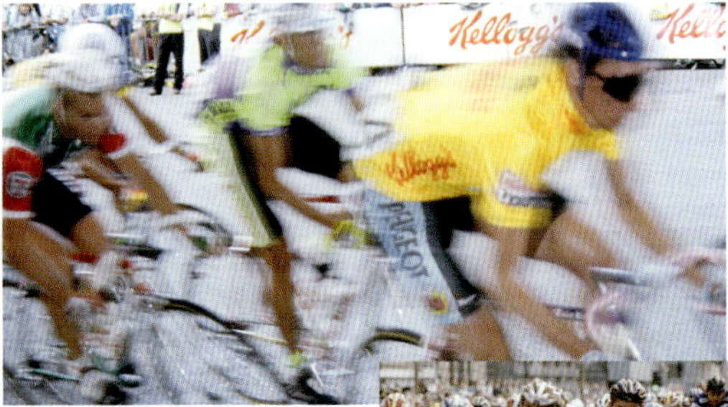

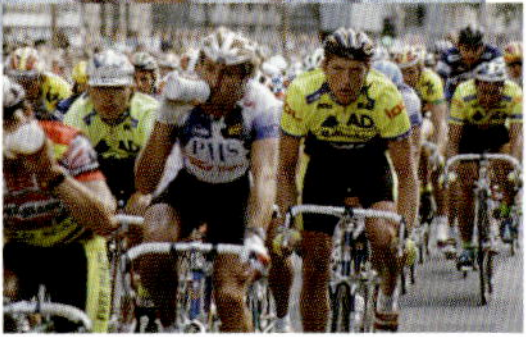

Some shots sum up the action much better than others. The telephoto shot of the cyclists shows the "peleton" well enough, but with two of the competitors choosing that moment to drink, it hardly looks like a race. The wide-angle shot works better. The use of slow-sync flash provides a feeling of movement, and the fact that the overall leader, in the yellow jersey, is in shot makes the picture more meaningful.

Aiming your sights

Although most DSLRs have autofocus systems that can keep up with moving subjects, and can even predict where they will move between the moment you press the shutter and the picture is taken, for many sports it is usually safer to use manual focus. The advantage is that you can set up the focus, and preframe the shot, even before the picture presents itself. This is because so many action events follow a predetermined course—and once your vantage point has been selected, you rarely have the chance to get more than one type of shot from it. Prefocus on a point through which you know the subject will pass, choosing a focal length to suit your distance from this point. When the subject comes into view, the focus is then set, and you can fire the shutter knowing you're in focus.

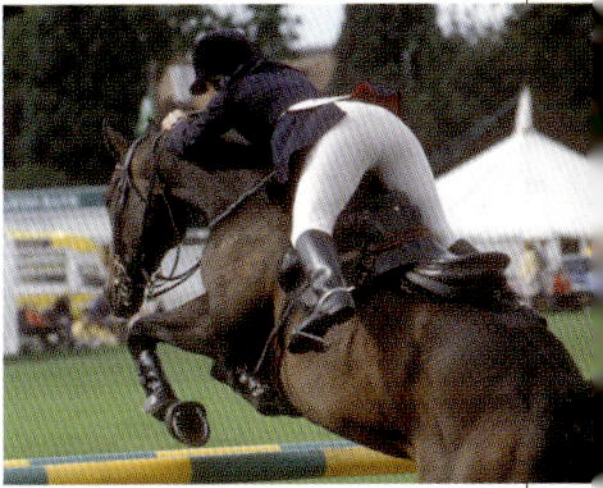

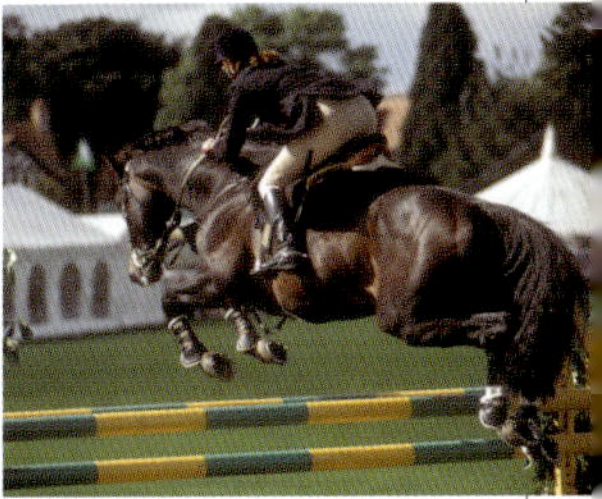

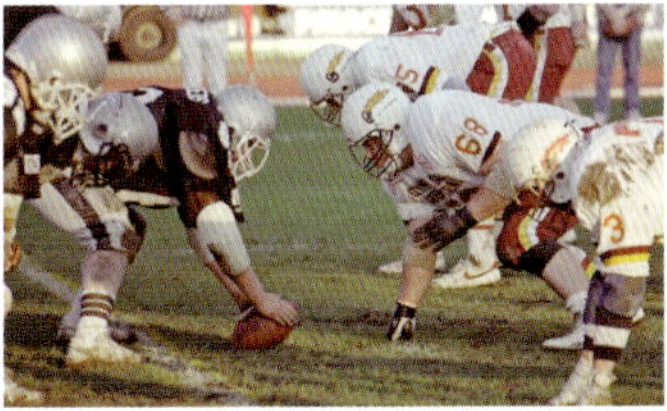

You don't need movement to create an action picture. As these two teams line up against one another, the tension is visible in the players' poses, helping capture the explosive nature of the game.

Photographing landscapes

Although wide-angle lenses have become almost synonymous with landscape photography—the wide outdoors demands wide angles of view—don't dismiss the possibility of using long focal-length settings. A telephoto allows you to isolate a distant tree, or home in on the pattern of fields or the diagonal line created by the side of a mountain.

The quality of the light is also of vital importance to the landscape photographer. The "golden hours" of early morning and late afternoon (depending on location and season) will often offer idyllic lighting conditions, but don't rule out other times of day or poor weather conditions—the creative landscape photographer will make the most of the least favorable conditions.

Finally, the seasons of course also play an important part in landscape photography; but again, successful landscapes don't necessarily rely on bright blue skies and fluffy white clouds. Winter can also be a wonderful time for graphic black and white shots.

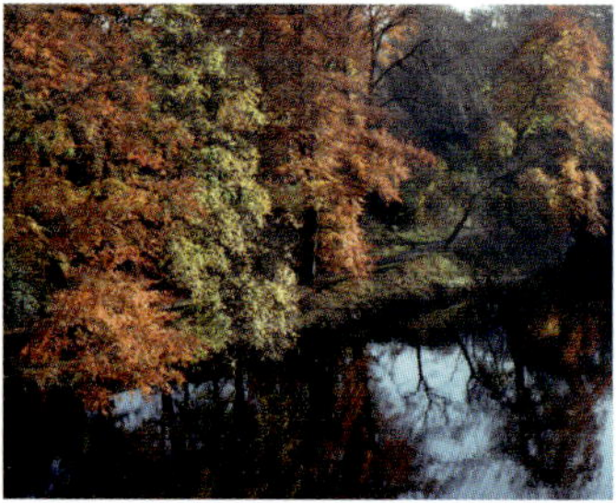

Water is a valuable ally for the landscape and garden photographer, reflecting the colors of the elements around it, as well as that of the sky.

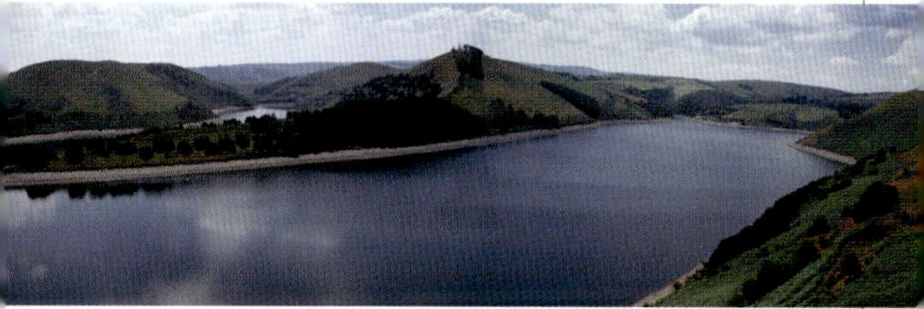

Although specialist cameras for shooting panoramas are available, it's relatively straightforward to combine a number of digital images to create a widescreen image. This panoramic approach allows you to photograph a broad vista without the need to include unnecessary foreground and sky, and without the need for an extreme wide-angle lens. Use a tripod and set the camera to manual so the exposure remains constant. Most image-editing software will then automatically stitch the images together to make the panorama.

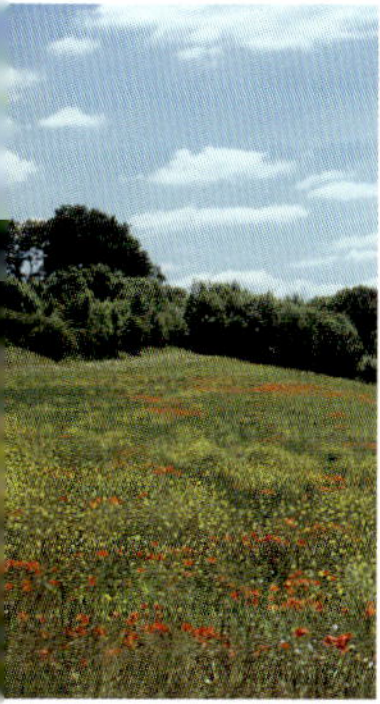

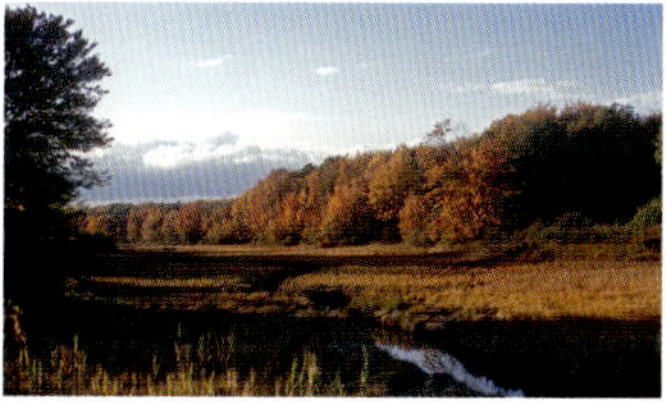

When shooting with a wide-angle lens it's essential to have plenty of foreground interest in a landscape shot, such as these poppies.

Late afternoon near Kennebunkport, Maine. The warm low light creates long shadows, and brings out the Fall colors of the maple trees.

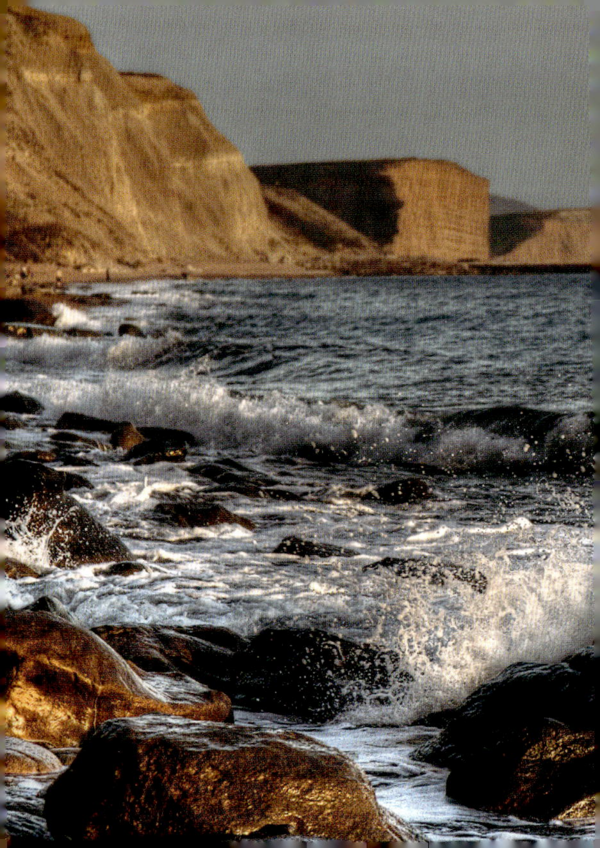

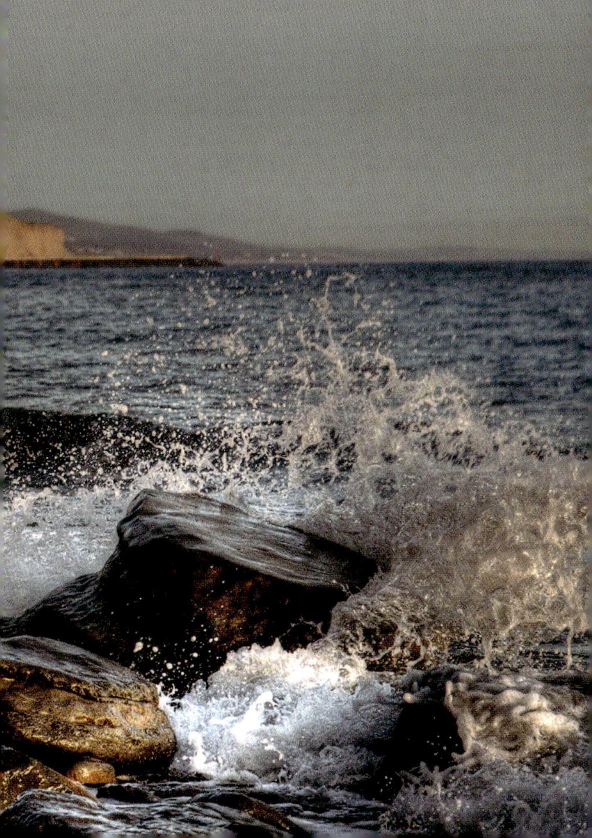

Photographing travel

While, on the one hand, travel photography offers a plethora of new sights and the time to photograph them, you're likely to be restricted as to the amount of equipment you can carry around with you. Tripods are cumbersome and long telephoto lenses heavy. Be prepared, you'll have to make difficult equipment choices before you leave. Most importantly, unless you're taking a laptop you need to estimate how many pictures you'll be taking (and more signficantly keeping) and make sure you have sufficient memory of one form or another—whether memory cards or a portable hard drive. Finally, consider power. You're likely to need at least two batteries and the relevant adaptor to run the charger.

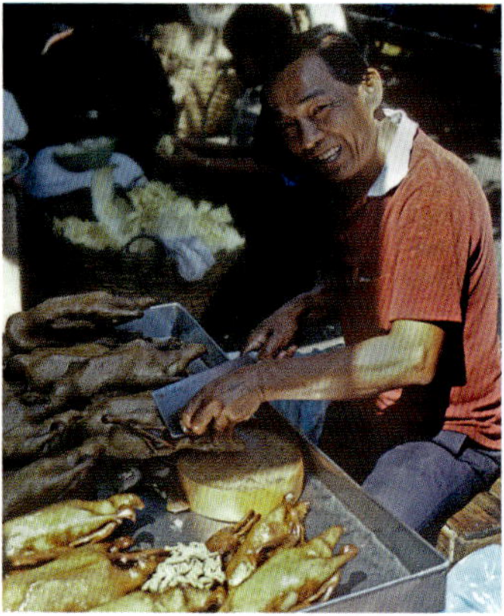

Duck being prepared on the street in Bangkok's Chinatown. Some destinations are undoubtedly better havens for photographers than others. Bustling Bangkok is certainly one of those destinations that has pictures at every corner. But you don't necessarily have to travel far to find these picture paradises.

Planning your time

- Use other people's pictures as a guide to the kind of shots that are possible. Look at guidebooks and websites to check the visual themes of a location before you leave.
- Postcards are a great source of inspiration, showing you views that you might otherwise not discover in a short stay. You don't have to copy them—try to improve on them or adapt them to your own style.
- Many of the most photogenic locations will also be the most popular with other tourists. Plan to arrive at the site as early as possible.
- Look out for details of events. Market days are often a photographer's paradise, for example, but these may only happen weekly.

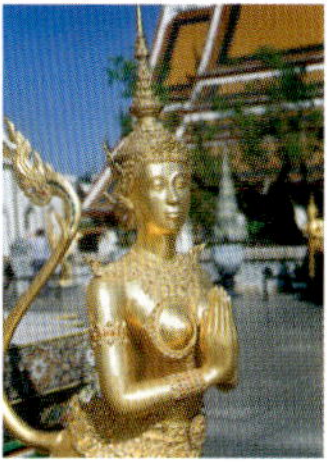

Remember to look out for detail as well as long shots.

The Giga Vu Sonic by Jobo features a 250Gb hard disk, a 3-inch (7.5-cm) high-resolution color display, and the ability to read most Raw format files as well as JPEGs. If you don't have access to a computer this may be the answer.

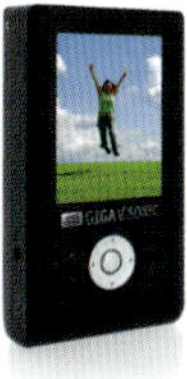

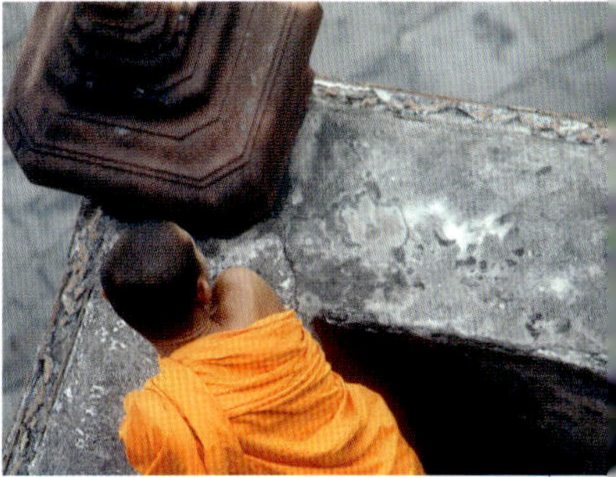

Candid shots of people, such as this one of a Buddhist monk, help to capture the essence of a foreign country. A medium telephoto zoom is ideal for this type of shot.

Macro photography

Macro photography opens up an entirely new world to the keen amateur photographer, and can quickly become a minor (or even a major) obsession. Under extreme close-up, almost everything you photograph, from plants and animals to inanimate objects, is seen from a new perspective.

For true macro photography, you need a macro lens. Such a lens will be capable of capturing an object at a scale of 1:1. A lot of lenses have a "macro" setting, but in reality these are likely only to be able to capture a scale of around 1:4. At this scale you'll be able to get good close-up shots, but not true macro.

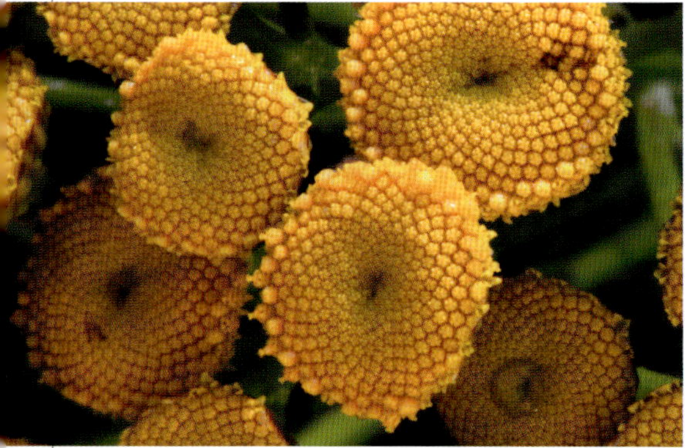

Macro photography is one of the best ways to explore the myriad of patterns found in the natural world, many of which are based on strict mathematical rules.

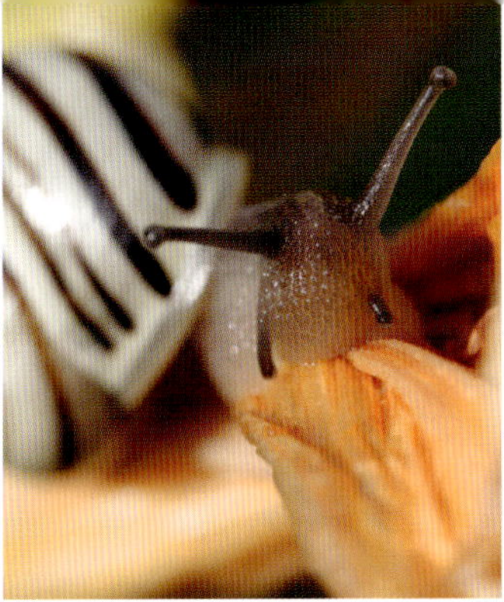

Narrow depth of field is a common occurrence with macro photography. Often you may find you have to decide what to keep in focus and what becomes blurred. It's much easier to focus manually, and take several shots to see which works best.

Whenever possible, frame the subject so that it shows up clearly against the background.

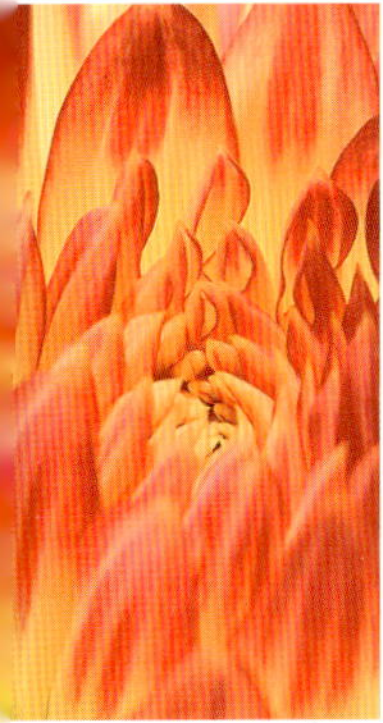

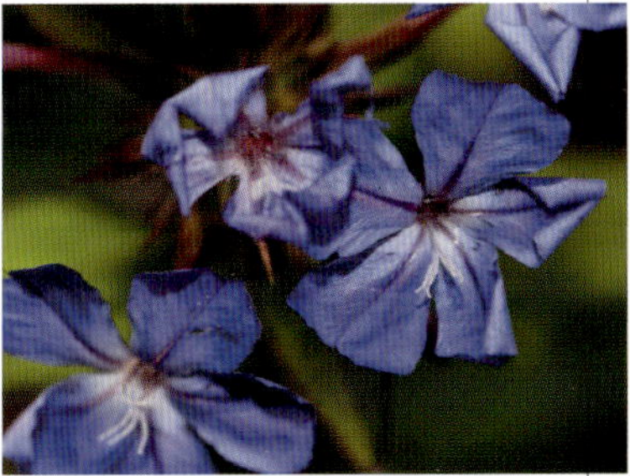

Dramatic, almost abstract, shots are easily achieved with a macro lens.

Using filters

Today's image-editing programs have, to a large degree, made most filters redundant, particularly those that were used for a specific creative effect. However there are a couple of filters, the effects of which cannot be replicated in the digital darkroom.

The first is the ultraviolet or UV filter. While you're unlikely to notice the difference between a shot taken with a UV filter and one taken without, the filter is invaluable for protecting the front element of the lens.

The next filter, the polarizer, has a much greater impact on the image. Polarizing filters cut out polarized light, that is light reflected off any shiny surface, such as glass or water. In this way, the filter can reduce reflections, haze and, under certain circumstances, boost color saturation. It's important to buy a "circular" polarizer, which you twist to get the appropriate angle depending on the direction the reflected light is entering the lens.

The final filter that can't be replicated on-computer is the graduated gray filter. As it's name suggests this filter is dark gray on one side fading to clear on the other. This allows you to "darken" a bright sky, helping to balance the exposure differential between sky and land.

Sometimes a polarizer can completely transform a scene. Here the two shots look as if they were taken in completely different lighting conditions—not just moments apart.

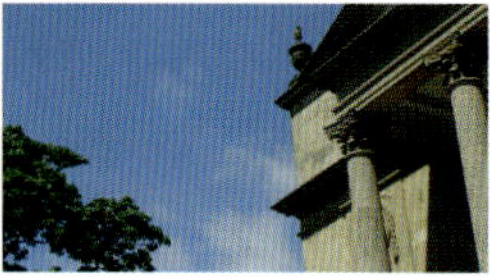

WITHOUT POLARIZER

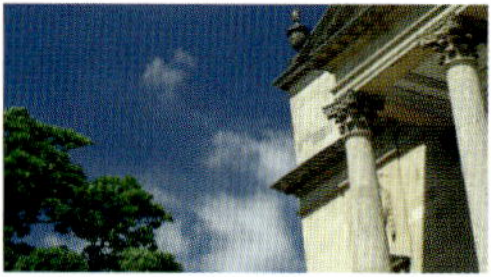

WITH POLARIZER

WITH POLARIZER

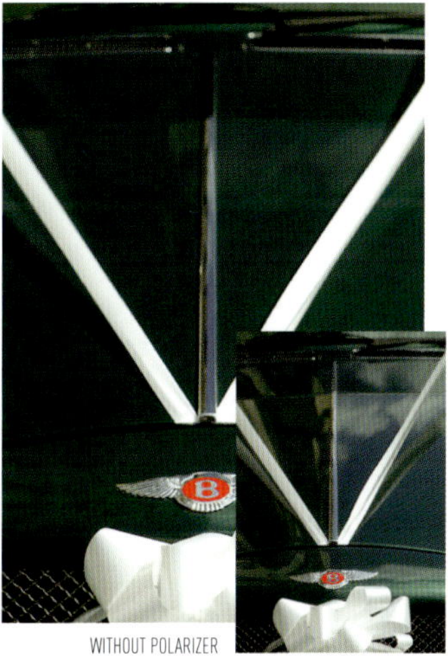

A circular polarizing filter is good at reducing reflections from glass and other shiny surfaces, such as the polished bonnet of this wedding car. Notice the absence of reflected clouds in the bigger image.

WITHOUT POLARIZER

The grad gray filter (below right) effectively darkens the upper part of the picture. This enables you to expose accurately for the land without overexposing the sky.

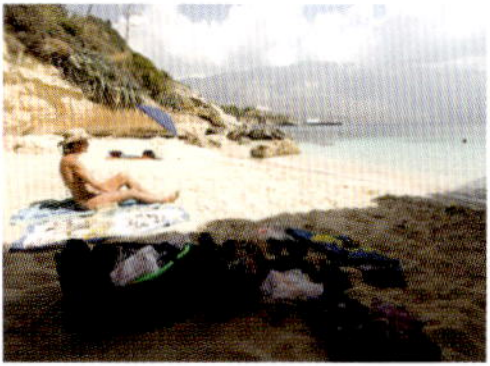

WITHOUT GRAY GRAD

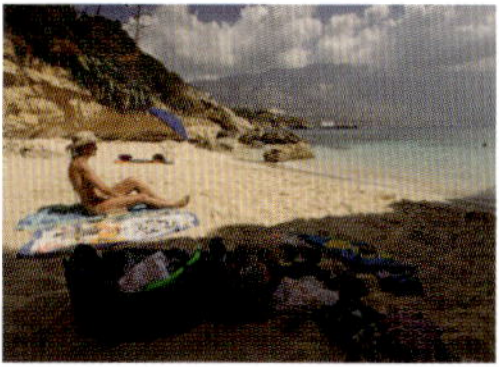

WITH GRAY GRAD

Frame your subject

Framing your subject can help to bring order to a composition and direct the viewer's eye to the subject of the photo. Frames can be natural or manmade, and applied to either landscape or portrait photography. It's important that the frame is sympathetic to the subject and not overly fussy or complicated or it will simply detract from the subject rather than bring the viewer in.

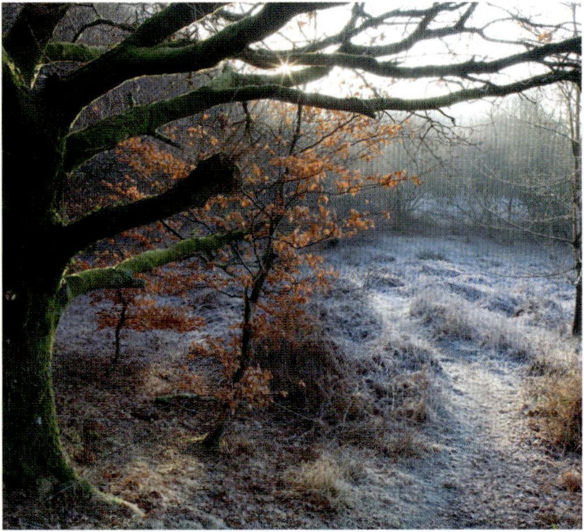

Trees are a common natural frame in landscape photography. As well providing a border to the image, they can also add depth to the image and so bring the viewer into the composition.

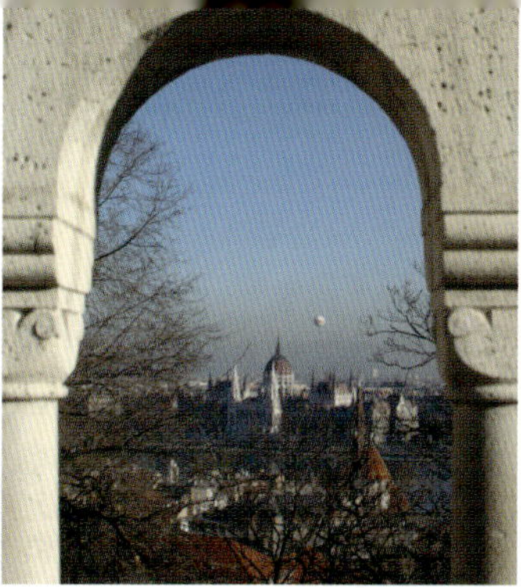

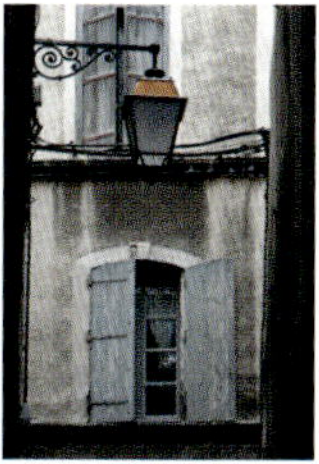

The walls of the narrow street in this southern French town help to frame the view of the shuttered windows beyond.

The arches in this shot taken in Budapest were deliberately blurred through the use of a wide aperture so that the viewer's attention is concentrated on the Hungarian Parliament buildings in the distance.

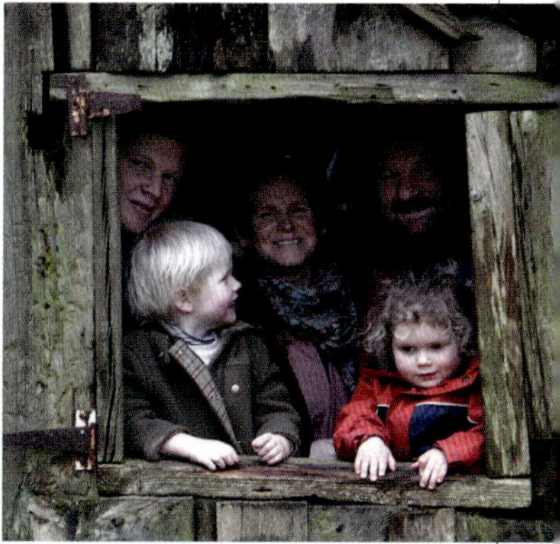

A window of a disused railway hut made a perfect frame within a frame in this group portrait.

Decide on the key

In most photographic situations, the composition is governed by the independent elements within the picture, and their relationship to one another. In such scenarios, the job of the photographer, having spotted the potential in the scene, is to capture the tones as accurately as possible. But there are other ways in which a composition can come about; one is through color, where the objects themselves are less important than their colors and the colors of other objects around them. A further driving factor is uniformity of tone. Occasionally, a scene will present itself to you, the tones of which are almost exclusively light (high key), or almost exclusively dark (low key). Such images can provoke a powerful response in the viewer. In order to maximize this response try to frame the scene so that the uniformity of tone is maintained as strongly as possible. It's then possible to exaggerate the effect during post-production.

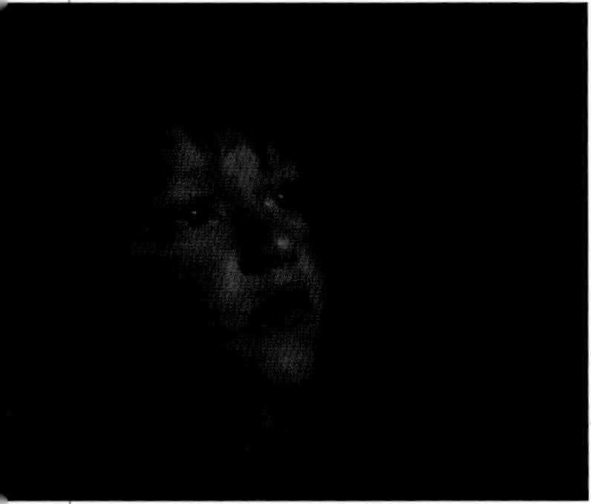

Low-key portraits can be successfully achieved using natural lighting from a single window, which is usually only bright enough to light a small area of the room, leaving most of the scene in darkness.

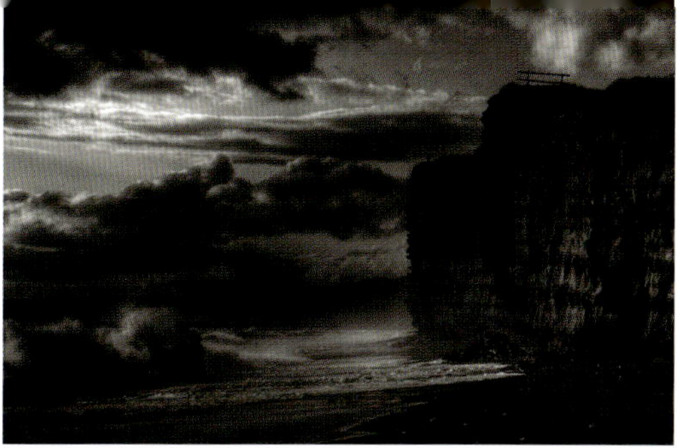

Low-key images are most effective when there are small but distinct areas of lighter tone to offset the generally somber mood. Here the image was converted to black and white.

A light sprinkling of snow and a steely gray sky provided the perfect conditions for this high-key landscape. Exposure compensation was set to + 2 to reinforce the lighter tones.

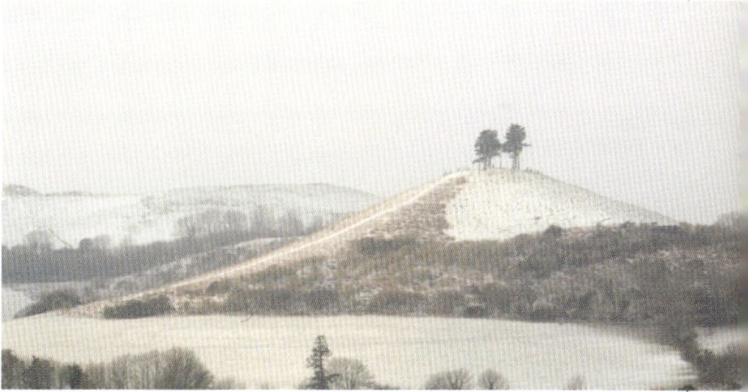

Glossary

AE Abbreviation of Automatic Exposure.

AEL Automatic Exposure Lock. A push-button control that lets you choose which part of the scene the camera takes its meter reading from, and then lock this setting while the image is reframed.

AF Abbreviation of Autofocus.

Angle of view A measurement of how much a lens can see of a scene from a particular position, usually measured in degrees. The longer the focal length of the lens, the smaller the angle of view. Zoom lenses have adjustable angles of view.

Aperture The opening in the lens that restricts how much light reaches the image sensor. In all but the most basic cameras, the size of the aperture is adjustable. The aperture setting used has an important role to play in both exposure and depth of field.

Aperture priority Semi-automatic exposure system, where the aperture is set by the photographer, and the shutter speed is then set by the camera to suit the light level reading taken by the camera's own meter.

Autofocus A system where the lens is adjusted automatically by the camera to bring the designated part of the image into sharp focus.

AWB (Automatic White Balance) System that automatically adjusts the color of the recorded picture so that it looks normal to the human eye.

B Abbreviation of Bulb. A shutter speed setting on a camera that allows you to keep the shutter open for as long as the shutter release is held down. Commonly used for long exposures.

Bracketing System for increasing the chances of getting the right exposure by taking a sequence of pictures with a slightly different exposure setting for each.

Camera shake Blurring of the image caused by movement of the camera during the exposure. Handheld cameras are prone to camera shake, and a fast shutter speed needs to be used to eliminate the problem.

Center-weighted Type of built-in metering system, provided as an option on some cameras. Center-weighted meters measure light intensity across the entire image area, but bias the average in favor of light taken toward the center of the frame.

Color temperature Measurement of the color of light, usually expressed in degrees Kelvin. The human eye adjusts automatically for color temperature much of the time, without us realizing; digital cameras can make electronic adjustments using their white balance systems to mimic the eye and brain.

Continuous autofocus AF setting where the focus is constantly adjusted until the shutter is actually fired. Useful for moving subjects, where it would be unhelpful for the focus distance to be locked as soon as initially found.

Depth of field A measure of how much of a picture is in focus, from the nearest point in the scene to the camera that looks sharp, to the furthermost point that looks sharp. Depth of field is dependent on the aperture used, the distance that the lens is focused at, and the focal length of the lens.

Dynamic range A measure of the range of image densities that can be recorded by a device, from its brightest white to its darkest black.

efl (effective focal length) Measure for comparison of the angle of view and magnification of different lenses and lens settings, whatever the size of imaging chip being used. The actual focal length is converted to the equivalent focal length that would give the same angle of view on a camera using 35mm film or a "full-frame" sensor.

Evaluative metering Metering system used on many cameras where light readings are taken from a number of different areas, or zones, across the image. These are then compared to data programmed into the camera, so it can work out an appropriate exposure setting. Information from the multipoint autofocus system is also used, to ascertain the likely position of the subject.

Exposure Total amount of light used to create an image.

Exposure compensation A control for manually overriding the built-in exposure meter of a camera to provide more or less light to the sensor.

f number The aperture setting. The number is the focal length of the lens divided by the diameter of the aperture; because of this, larger f numbers represent smaller aperture sizes.

f stop See f number.

File format The way in which a digital file is saved. A digital image can be saved in a wide variety of different file formats, the most commonly used being Raw and JPEG. The format dictates which programs will be able to read and open the file. It also dictates the amount of information and the detail that is stored. Other formats include TIFF, EPS, and GIF.

Fill-in flash Flash used as a secondary lightsource. A fill-flash feature is an option on many cameras with a built-in flash unit, letting you soften shadows on foreground subjects or enhance the colors and contrast of foreground subjects in dull lighting conditions.

Focal length An optical term describing the distance between the optical center of a lens and its focal point. In practice, the focal length of a lens is a measure of the magnification and angle of view of a given lens or zoom setting. It is usually measured in millimeters.

Highlight The brightest areas of an image—the white areas in a picture.

Histogram Graph used as a way of depicting the brightness, tonal range, and contrast of an image during digital manipulation. Also used as a way of evaluating exposure by some cameras.

JPEG (Joint Photographic Experts Group) A file format used widely for digital images. A variable amount of compression can be used to vary the amount of detail stored and the resulting file size. It is the standard format used by digital cameras (although Raw or TIFF formats may also be provided as options).

Low key An image that is dominated by dark tones.

Macro Term generally used to describe equipment or a facility for taking pictures at a closer shooting distance than usual, to provide a bigger image of the subject. Historically speaking the term macro refers to when the recorded image is lifesize or larger, with a magnification ratio that is 1:1 or greater.

Manual exposure Exposure mode where both shutter speed and aperture are set by the photographer.

Matrix metering See Evaluative metering.

Megapixel Measurement of the resolution of a digital camera, equal to 1,000,000 pixels.

Metered manual Exposure mode where, although shutter speed and aperture are set manually by the user, information as to their suitability is provided by the camera's own metering system.

Multizone metering See Evaluative metering.

Neutral density (ND) Optical or electronic filter that reduces the amount of light reaching the image sensor equally across the entire field of view. It permits longer shutter speeds or wider apertures than would otherwise be possible in the lighting conditions.

Noise Unwanted interference in an electrical signal. Seen as a grain-like pattern in dark areas of a digital image, noise increases when a higher ISO setting is used.

Partial metering Type of metering system where the exposure reading is taken from a small area in the center of the field of view, similar to spot metering, but covering a slightly larger area of the image.

Predictive autofocus Sophisticated autofocus setting where the focus is not only adjusted until the shutter is actually fired, but continues to be adjusted during the delay between pressing the shutter and the picture being taken.

Prefocusing Manual focusing technique used for moving subjects. The lens is focused on a point or at a distance which you anticipate the subject will move through. The shutter is released when this point is reached.

Program exposure Any exposure mode where the camera sets both the aperture and the shutter speed automatically.

Program shift Program exposure mode where the camera sets the shutter speed and aperture automatically, but the photographer has the option of altering the bias between the two readings to set a preferred shutter speed or aperture without changing the overall exposure.

Raw A native file format offered by some digital cameras. Image data is stored in a semi-processed state and must be fully processed on a computer. Enables exposure compensation and color balance to be altered after camera exposure, and typically provides a 16-bit color depth option.

Rear curtain sync Flash feature found on some digital SLRs and flashguns that synchronizes the flash output when the second shutter curtain is about to close. Usually, the flash fires at the point where the first shutter is fully open. The facility gives more natural-looking images when using flash in conjunction with slow shutter speeds.

Resolution The measure of a lens or digital-imaging device's ability to record fine detail.

Shutter priority Semi-automatic exposure mode where the shutter speed is set by the photographer, and the aperture is then set by the camera to suit the metered light readings taken by the camera.

Spot metering Exposure metering system where a meter reading is taken from a very small area in the center of the frame.

Stop A unit of exposure. Changing exposure by a single stop is equivalent to doubling or halving the amount of light reaching the image sensor. The distance between each of the standard aperture settings (f2.8, f4, f 5.6, f 8, etc) is a full stop.

TIFF (Tagged Image File Format) Digital image format used to record files with maximum available detail. Files can be large, although this can be reduced using "lossless" compression.

Tv (Time Value) Abbreviation used for shutter priority on some cameras.

UV filter Optical filter that absorbs ultraviolet (UV) radiation. The filter can be used to improve visibility and quality in mountain and maritime landscapes.

White balance Digital camera system that sets the color temperature for the scene being photographed. This can be set automatically, with the system attempting to set the color so that it looks neutral to the human eye. Many cameras also offer preset and custom white balance settings.

Zoom A lens with a variable angle of view.

Index

Picture Credits

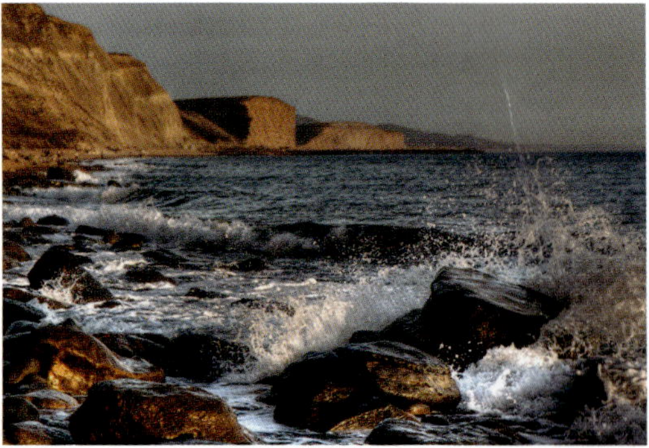

Will Cheung 34–35, 72, 73

Chris George 2, 8, 14, 15, 16, 17, 18–19, 25, 27, 29, 31, 32, 32, 36, 37, 38, 39, 40, 41 (left, bottom), 42, 43, 44, 45, 47 (bottom), 51, 58, 59, 64, 65, 66, 67, 68, 69, 70, 71 (middle), 77, 79 (top left, bottom), 80, 81 (middle, bottom), 82, 83, 84 (left), 85 (bottom left, bottom right), 91, 94, 95, 98, 99, 101, 102, 103, 104, 105, 108, 109, 112, 113 (top)

Steve Luck
7, 11, 13, 20, 21, 23, 41 (right), 46, 47 (top, middle), 48–49, 50, 53, 55, 57, 60–61, 62, 63, 71 (top, bottom), 74–75, 76, 78, 79 (top right), 81 (top), 84 (right), 85 (top), 86–87, 88, 89, 90, 92, 93, 96–97, 100, 106–107, 110, 111, 113 (bottom), 114, 115, 116, 117, 118–119